Conquests in Reading

Second Edition

William Kottmeyer
Formerly Superintendent of Schools
St. Louis, Missouri

Phoenix Learning Resources
New York

Copyright © 1989, 1962 by Phoenix Learning Resources, Inc. All Rights Reserved. No part of this publication may be reproduced, stored in a retrieval system, in any form or by any means, electronic, mechanical, photocopying, recording, or otherwise, without the prior written permission of the publisher. Printed in the United States of America.

ISBN 0-7915-2404-3

UNIT 1

Consonant Sounds

These are consonant sounds. Learn the sounds and the picture words. When your teacher gives you the name of the consonant, tell which picture goes with it. When your teacher shows the picture, tell the consonant sound.

b spells the sound that starts

c spells the sound that starts

d spells the sound that starts

f spells the sound that starts

g spells the sound that starts

h spells the sound that starts

j spells the sound that starts

k spells the sound that starts

l spells the sound that starts

m spells the sound that starts

UNIT 1

Consonant Sounds

Here are more consonant sounds.

n spells the sound that starts

p spells the sound that starts

r spells the sound that starts

s spells the sound that starts

t spells the sound that starts

v spells the sound that starts

w spells the sound that starts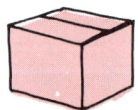

x spells the <u>ks</u> sound that ends

y spells the sound that starts

z spells the sound that starts

UNIT 1

Consonant Sounds

Write the consonant sounds on the lines.

UNIT 1

Consonant Sounds

Write the consonant letter that starts each picture word.

1. _____ 2. _____ 3. _____ 4. _____ 5. _____

6. _____ 7. _____ 8. _____ 9. _____ 10. _____

11. _____ 12. _____ 13. _____ 14. _____ 15. _____

16. _____ 17. _____ 18. _____ 19. _____ 20. _____

21. _____ 22. _____ 23. _____ 24. _____ 25. _____

26. _____ 27. _____ 28. _____ 29. _____ 30. _____

31. _____ 32. _____ 33. _____ 34. _____ 35. _____

36. _____ 37. _____ 38. _____ 39. _____ 40. _____

UNIT 1

Consonant Sounds

Write the consonant letter that starts each picture word.

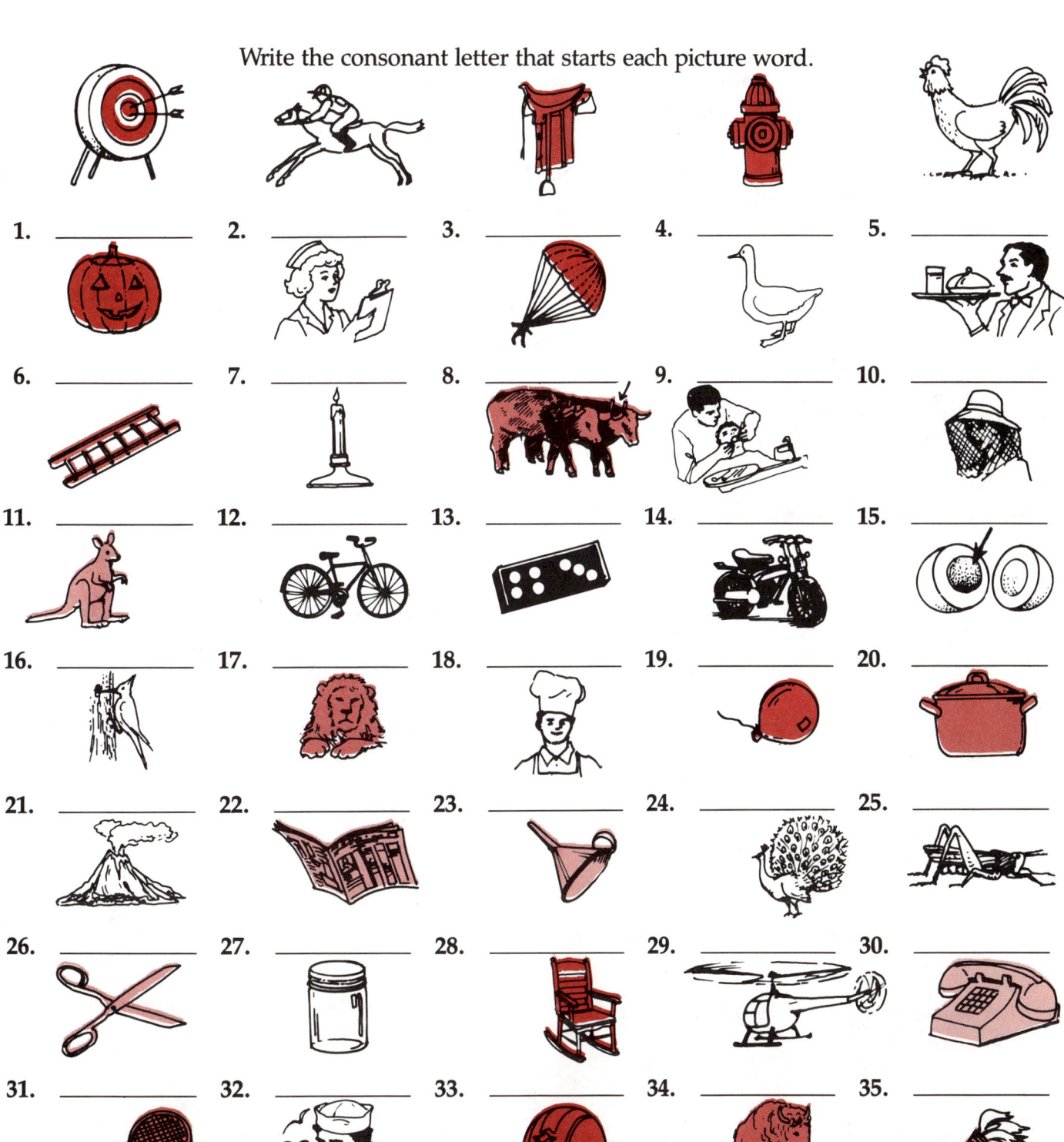

UNIT 2

Sounding a Words

The **a** is a vowel. It has the sound that starts **apple**. Read these words. Say the sounds softly together to say each word.

a is the sound that starts

SIGHT WORDS
of the have does who to are do there you

lap	ham	fast	have*
bag	cab	lad	nap
fan	and	ran	rap
of*	pat	last	wag
bat	sap	do*	tap
cat	hat	rag	tan
bad	cap	mad	to*
an	land	pan	band
fat	the*	mat	tag
does*	gas	sand	pal
at	ask	sad	clap
am	add	you*	there*
dad	lamp	man	slap
had	who*	sat	back
can	camp	map	pad
are*	hand	rat	past

*Sight words

UNIT 2

Spelling a Words

Say the picture words. Hear the sounds. Spell the words by writing letters for the sounds you hear.

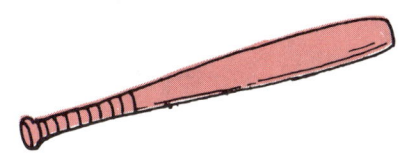 

1. _____   2. _____   3. _____

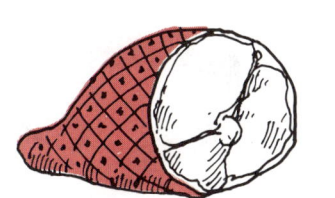 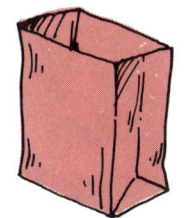 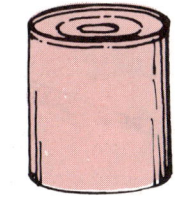

4. _____   5. _____   6. _____

7. _____   8. _____   9. _____

10. _____ 11. _____ 12. _____

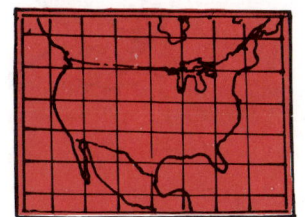  

13. _____ 14. _____ 15. _____

7

UNIT 2

Spelling a Words

What are they?

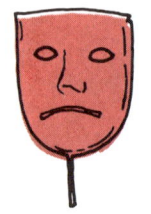

1. _____   2. _____   3. _____

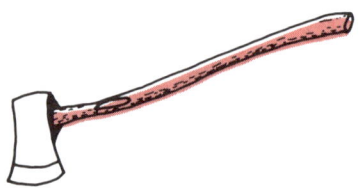

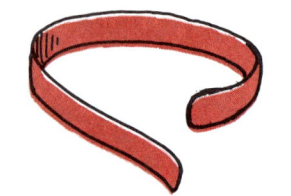

4. _____   5. _____   6. _____

What do they do?

7. _____   8. _____   9. _____

How do they look?

10. _____   11. _____   12. _____

UNIT 2

Reading Sentences

Read the sentences. Draw a line under **yes** or **no**.

1. Are land maps flat? — Yes — No
2. Are there cats who are black? — Yes — No
3. Can you trap rats? — Yes — No
4. Can a man hand you a bat? — Yes — No
5. Does a cat have hands? — Yes — No
6. Can a man grab an ax? — Yes — No
7. Do you have flags at camp? — Yes — No
8. Can you tack slats to a raft? — Yes — No
9. Can you clap hands? — Yes — No
10. Do ramps slant? — Yes — No
11. Can you drag rafts to land? — Yes — No
12. Do rat traps snap fast? — Yes — No
13. Can you have lamps at camp? — Yes — No
14. Can a fat lad have cramps? — Yes — No
15. Can you wag a flag? — Yes — No
16. Can you ask a pal to bat last? — Yes — No
17. Can you add bags and bats? — Yes — No
18. Do you have gas lamps at camp? — Yes — No
19. Are rats as fast as cats? — Yes — No
20. Does a ham have fat? — Yes — No
21. Can a lad's cap have flaps? — Yes — No
22. Do hats have black bands? — Yes — No
23. Do you have to have a flag at camp? — Yes — No
24. Does a man have to have a gas mask? — Yes — No
25. Can a man blast sand? — Yes — No

UNIT 3

Sounding i Words

The **i** is a vowel. It has the sound that starts **igloo**. Read these words. Say the sounds softly together to say each word.

i is the sound that starts

SIGHT WORDS
one buy move from some should want two they only

is	bill	till	lit
rid	rim	dim	pin
it	want*	mill	fill
risk	hill	miss	move*
dig	tip	some*	fit
hip	hid	if	lift
his	bib	silk	kiss
him	sip	rip	fist
one*	milk	pill	kill
did	rib	limp	should*
hit	big	pig	fin
from*	bid	two*	hint
dip	in	lip	will
tin	ill	lid	wig
sit	buy*	pit	they*
sift	bit	only*	win

*Sight words

10

UNIT 3

Sounding a and i Words

Say the sounds softly together to say the words.

a is the sound that starts

i is the sound that starts

SIGHT WORDS
have you do who there of are to the does

crack	stick	tick	do*
twist	are*	grass	cliff
clamp	cramp	spin	drip
drift	fact	draft	snap
glad	grand	to*	flip
have*	flag	spill	grip
blast	drill	grab	of*
twig	brass	strip	black
brand	skim	drag	slim
stiff	you*	does*	stack
slid	clam	skip	still
who*	split	flat	slick
crab	brag	trip	the*
slip	trim	flap	track
brick	graft	brat	trick
twin	there*	class	grin

*Sight words

11

UNIT 3

Spelling i Words

Say the picture words. Hear the sounds. Spell the words by writing letters for the sounds you hear.

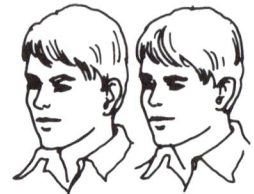  

1. _____ 2. _____ 3. _____

4. _____ 5. _____ 6. _____

7. _____ 8. _____ 9. _____

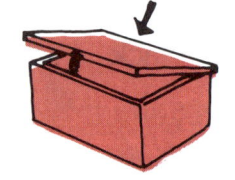 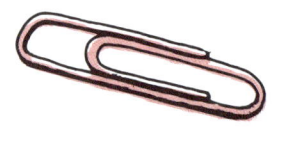 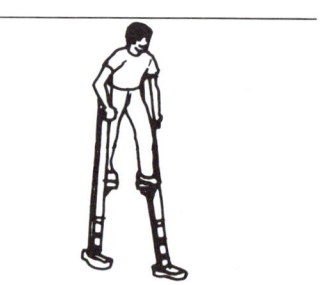

10. _____ 11. _____ 12. _____

13. _____ 14. _____ 15. _____

UNIT 3

Adding Word Endings

Say the words in the boxes.

can	cats	bat	bag
cans	cat	bats	bags
lid	pin	fists	ribs
lids	pins	fist	rib
lamp	hips	hats	hill
lamps	hip	hat	hills
land	risk	asked	hinting
lands	risks	asks	hinted
landed	risked	asking	hint
landing	risking	ask	hints
camps	limps	hand	lift
camped	limp	hands	lifts
camp	limped	handing	lifted
camping	limping	handed	lifting
killing	add	fill	lasting
killed	adding	fills	lasted
kill	adds	filling	lasts
kills	added	filled	last

UNIT 3

Reading Sentences

Read the sentences. Draw a line under **yes** or **no**.

1.	Do flags flap in a stiff wind?	Yes	No
2.	Can you stick some pins in bricks?	Yes	No
3.	Does one slip in slick grass?	Yes	No
4.	Will you limp if you have a bad cramp?	Yes	No
5.	Can you spin a tin can lid?	Yes	No
6.	Do they buy gas only in cans?	Yes	No
7.	Do cats want to kill rats?	Yes	No
8.	Can you dig a pit in the sand?	Yes	No
9.	Can you slip if you are limping?	Yes	No
10.	Should bands drill if they are ill?	Yes	No
11.	Should you skip class if you are sick?	Yes	No
12.	Do cabs skid if the bricks are slick?	Yes	No
13.	Can a slim man grip a bat in his fists?	Yes	No
14.	Are there pigs who have only two ribs?	Yes	No
15.	Do you have to have fins to swim?	Yes	No
16.	Can you pin a band to the brim of a hat?	Yes	No
17.	Do you lick a stamp to have it stick?	Yes	No
18.	Will you spill the milk if you tilt the glass?	Yes	No
19.	Are Jack and Jill the two who slipped?	Yes	No
20.	Can you move the lid from a milk can?	Yes	No
21.	Are sticks big stiff twigs?	Yes	No
22.	Can you lift a big milk can?	Yes	No
23.	Should you stick to the facts?	Yes	No
24.	Do big kids still sip milk?	Yes	No
25.	Should a big brass band have drills?	Yes	No

UNIT 4

Sounding u Words

The **u** is a vowel. It has the sound that starts **umbrella**. Read these words. Say the sounds softly together to say each word.

u is the sound that starts

SIGHT WORDS
come any none one both
was would been put done

hub	bum	runt	muss
rug	bump	dump	tug
come*	dust	been*	lump
us	bun	mud	was*
hump	bus	pup	gum
hum	hut	cuff	gun
mumps	tub	cup	rust
rub	must	done*	suds
but	mug	nut	puff
one*	any*	cub	tuck
dug	fund	cut	put*
run	fun	pump	dull
up	bug	hug	bunt
rut	sum	fuss	sulk
would*	bud	none*	luck
sun	both*	lug	duck

*Sight words

UNIT 4

Sounding a, i, and u Words

Say the sounds softly together to say the words.

a is the sound that starts

i is the sound that starts

u is the sound that starts

SIGHT WORDS
want buy from some should one only move were they

glad	drug	stag	kick
tilt	slacks	pick	plug
buck	only*	stuck	scalp
brad	swift	move*	grill
sick	skull	tusk	strut
want*	sank	flip	brag
blunt	swim	stunt	blink
sack	crust	they*	two*
pulp	buy*	stand	grunt
stump	grand	print	draft
drank	skid	slug	slump
some*	struck	spank	plum
drip	snap	clip	were*
bluff	lick	spun	brand
raft	should*	from*	mint
skin	drum	stab	stub

*Sight words

16

UNIT 4

Spelling u Words

Say the picture words. Hear the sounds. Write the words.

1. _____   2. _____   3. _____

4. _____   5. _____   6. _____

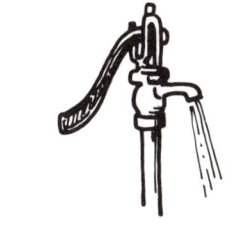

7. _____   8. _____   9. _____

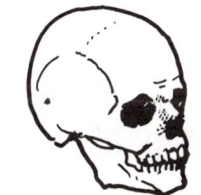

10. _____   11. _____   12. _____

13. _____   14. _____   15. _____

17

Words and Meanings

In each set of four words, one word does not belong. Draw a line under the word that does not belong.

1.	bud	fist	hand	lip
2.	plum	fig	bump	nut
3.	ant	grub	bug	sack
4.	stilt	stick	bat	drum
5.	bus	pig	cat	pup
6.	lump	cap	hat	muff
7.	bus	truck	dust	cab
8.	tramp	bump	lump	hump
9.	hip	pump	rib	back
10.	run	jump	swim	skip
11.	slap	smack	slug	mud
12.	drum	snap	crack	split
13.	clip	snip	bunt	cut
14.	add	stump	plus	sum
15.	brisk	nag	fast	swift
16.	scum	mud	muck	glass
17.	fat	two	one	six
18.	trust	bulb	switch	plug
19.	pup	cut	pig	duck
20.	punt	kick	cup	pass

UNIT 5

Sounding e Words

The **e** is a vowel. It has the sound that starts **elephant**. Read these words. Say the sounds softly together to say each word.

e is the sound that starts

SIGHT WORDS
gone said their people could
friend give many your work

red	mend	could*	felt
bend	give*	fell	their*
rest	belt	let	ten
sent	kept	fed	end
bell	best	tent	get
gone*	pen	lend	dent
bent	bet	many*	friend*
hem	held	left	wet
pet	rent	neck	desk
mess	beg	tell	went
people*	met	led	net
bed	said*	nest	well
melt	help	work*	your*
pest	set	less	web
send	hen	test	elm
men	sell	west	pelt

*Sight words

21

UNIT 5

Sounding a, i, u and e Words

Say the sounds softly together to say the words.

a is the sound that starts

i is the sound that starts

u is the sound that starts

e is the sound that starts

SIGHT WORDS
both any put would come
were done none been was

smell	cluck	spent	put*
strap	press	none*	crept
grin	swell	hint	slum
both*	any*	fan	kid
plum	tramp	task	glad
bled	club	mad	were*
spend	bless	drift	dress
slant	click	grab	stun
would*	plump	was*	wed
film	stem	tend	drip
suck	come*	weld	den
step	nick	sled	been*
stamp	slept	grub	stump
done*	tack	kiss	peck
speck	swept	wag	blend
grip	bluff	deck	dad

*Sight words

UNIT 5

Spelling e Words

Say the picture words. Hear the sounds. Write the words.

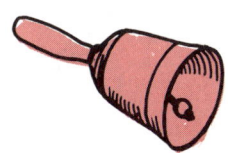 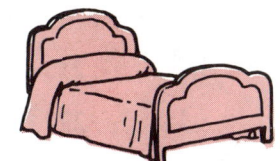 

1. _____ 2. _____ 3. _____

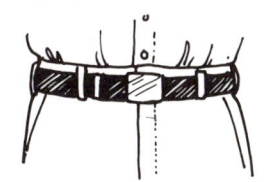  

4. _____ 5. _____ 6. _____

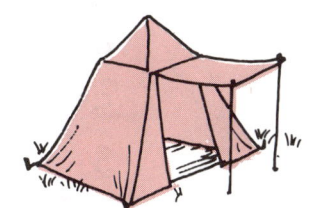  

7. _____ 8. _____ 9. _____

 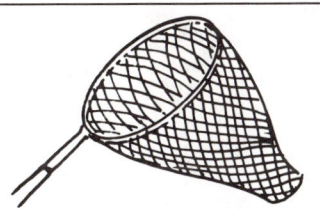 

10. _____ 11. _____ 12. _____

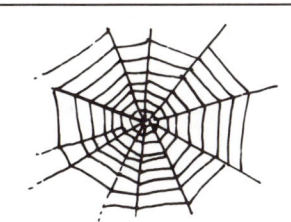 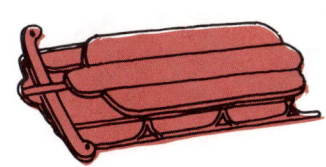 

13. _____ 14. _____ 15. _____

UNIT 5

Words and Meanings

If a pair of words mean about the same, mark **S**. If they are opposite, mark **O**.

1.	damp—wet	S	O	21.	spent—kept	S	O
2.	little—big	S	O	22.	glad—sad	S	O
3.	sick—ill	S	O	23.	blend—mix	S	O
4.	glum—sad	S	O	24.	from—to	S	O
5.	snip—cut	S	O	25.	walk—run	S	O
6.	slim—fat	S	O	26.	send—get	S	O
7.	skid—slip	S	O	27.	mend—fix	S	O
8.	sell—buy	S	O	28.	rested—slept	S	O
9.	mud—muck	S	O	29.	kick—punt	S	O
10.	stunt—trick	S	O	30.	sack—bag	S	O
11.	sick—well	S	O	31.	stand—sit	S	O
12.	plump—slim	S	O	32.	bump—lump	S	O
13.	tilt—slant	S	O	33.	ask—tell	S	O
14.	miss—hit	S	O	34.	crack—split	S	O
15.	sniff—smell	S	O	35.	trim—clip	S	O
16.	stiff—limp	S	O	36.	stub—end	S	O
17.	swift—fast	S	O	37.	pluck—pick	S	O
18.	bum—tramp	S	O	38.	sniff—smell	S	O
19.	dull—blunt	S	O	39.	hit—slap	S	O
20.	plump—fat	S	O	40.	vast—little	S	O

UNIT 5

Reading Sentences

Read the sentences. Draw a line under **yes** or **no**.

1.	Could you get your dented pens mended?	Yes	No
2.	Could a plump red hen have slept in a nest?	Yes	No
3.	Would people have been well rested in wet beds?	Yes	No
4.	Have many men slept in their tents?	Yes	No
5.	Would you want to give your pet cat the best milk?	Yes	No
6.	Have you done the best spelling tests in your class?	Yes	No
7.	Can you mend the hems on red dresses?	Yes	No
8.	Is six less two plus one less than ten?	Yes	No
9.	Could you press a dress if it were still wet?	Yes	No
10.	Could many big kids get any rest in one bed?	Yes	No
11.	Would wax tend to melt if you put it in the sun?	Yes	No
12.	Would you want your pet hen to be well fed?	Yes	No
13.	Does the sun set in the west?	Yes	No
14.	Would you have said yes if your friend wanted help?	Yes	No
15.	Do desks still have ink wells?	Yes	No
16.	Would you work to help your best friend?	Yes	No
17.	Do some men both buy and sell stamps?	Yes	No
18.	Does your dad send his slacks to get pressed?	Yes	No
19.	Must one have help to get eggs from the hen's nest?	Yes	No
20.	Would you spend less if you have lots of cash?	Yes	No

UNIT 6

Sounding o Words

The **o** is a vowel. It has the sound that starts **octopus**. Read these words. Say the sounds softly together to say each word.

o is the sound that starts

SIGHT WORDS
most live very what other
break where watch through once

odd	mop	sod	drop
hop	dock	sock	flop
dot	nod	on	block
pond	lock	watch*	slop
most*	bond	lop	break*
lot	not	pop	flock
doll	rob	tot	hock
cot	live*	once*	bob
pot	rot	mock	cog
what*	rod	pod	lob
fond	top	smock	crock
mob	God	sop	through*
cop	rock	gob	smog
where*	other*	stop	romp
cob	got	spot	fob
hot	sob	very*	cod

*Sight words

UNIT 6

Sounding a, i, u, e, and o Words

Say the sounds together to say the words.

a is the sound that starts    i is the sound that starts    u is the sound that starts

e is the sound that starts    o is the sound that starts

SIGHT WORDS
gone said your people could
their give many friend work

plot	trust	gasp	slam
trap	give*	drill	step
crisp	crept	bulb	their*
plus	crop	many*	blob
gone*	swam	wed	raft
spell	wilt	blot	still
clot	trunk	stack	clod
prop	wept	drip	stunt
plan	trot	work*	west
people*	scalp	must	plod
cliff	said*	left	friend*
truck	wind	slot	flat
fled	suds	clap	flip
clock	dress	your*	blunt
smack	could*	stock	blend
wick	blond	strip	plop

*Sight words

UNIT 6

Spelling o Words

Say the picture words. Hear the sounds. Write the words.

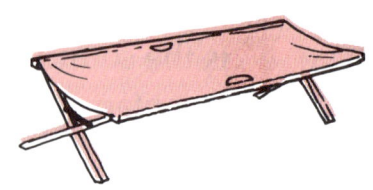
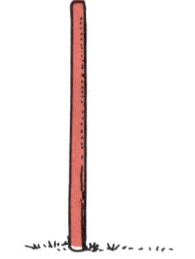

1. _____ 2. _____ 3. _____

4. _____ 5. _____ 6. _____

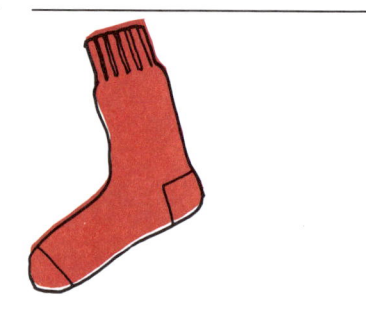

7. _____ 8. _____ 9. _____

10. _____ 11. _____ 12. _____

13. _____ 14. _____ 15. _____

28

UNIT 7

More Consonant Sounds

sh spells the sound that starts **sh**oe and ends fi**sh**

ch spells the sound that starts **ch**air and ends ben**ch**

tch spells the *ch* ending.

SIGHT WORDS
front full great taste waste weigh weighs sight change strange

SIGHT WORDS
door father mother head wash water eye young talk walk

ship	fresh	check	rich	ditch
shot	trash	chest	bunch	stretch
front*	cash	door*	inch	hatch
shin	weigh*	chat	ranch	stitch
shrimp	flush	chap	walk*	crutch
full*	dash	chew	branch	patch
shut	weight*	eye*	bench	pitch
shift	mash	chop	pinch	notch
great*	crush	chick	wash*	latch
shell	hush	father*	such	fetch
shelf	eight*	chill	much	catch
taste	mush	chin	lunch	itch
shock	blush	chum	water*	witch
shabby	flash	mother*	gulch	clutch
shark	change*	chip	punch	match
waste*	plush	checkers	drench	Dutch
shaft	gush	chimp	head*	Scotch
shaggy	rush	chuck	young*	blotch
shiver	strange*	talk*	crunch	snitch
shred	hash	chubby	trench	hitch
shrill	flesh	chiggers	munch	sketch
shun	crash	choppy	mulch	watch

*Sight words

UNIT 7

Spelling sh and (t)ch Words

Say the picture words. Hear the sounds. Write the words.

 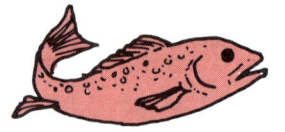 

1. _____ 2. _____ 3. _____

4. _____ 5. _____ 6. _____

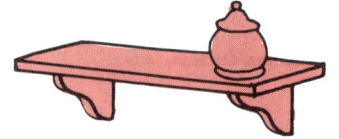  

7. _____ 8. _____ 9. _____

  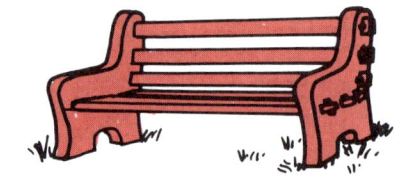

10. _____ 11. _____ 12. _____

13. _____ 14. _____ 15. _____

UNIT 7

Spelling th, wh, and ng Words

Say the picture words. Hear the sounds. Write the words.

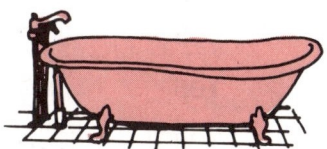   10th   5th

1. _____ 2. _____ 3. _____

6th

4. _____ 5. _____ 6. _____

   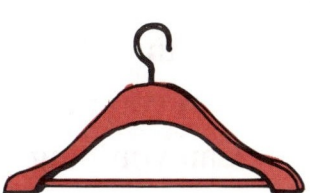

7. _____ 8. _____ 9. _____

   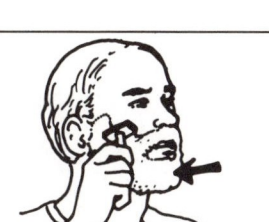   

10. _____ 11. _____ 12. _____

13. _____ 14. _____ 15. _____

35

UNIT 7

Reading Sentences

Read the sentences. Draw a line under **yes** or **no**.

1.	Are any of your friends a whiz at ping pong?	Yes	No
2.	Would moths bother a thick cloth quilt in a chest?	Yes	No
3.	Would you rather sing songs than do your math work?	Yes	No
4.	Is the width of a path very much less than its length?	Yes	No
5.	Is one fifth of a thing less than one tenth of it?	Yes	No
6.	Does a thrush have only one wing?	Yes	No
7.	Does a fish have lungs?	Yes	No
8.	Can you hang your slacks on a hanger?	Yes	No
9.	Do thrifty people spend their cash quickly?	Yes	No
10.	Can you tell whether a ring was once chipped?	Yes	No
11.	Could a man with long whiskers trim them?	Yes	No
12.	Would your pup whimper when you pinched it?	Yes	No
13.	Do you bother your class when you whisper?	Yes	No
14.	Is having two kings better than one?	Yes	No
15.	Must you have great strength to thump a drum?	Yes	No
16.	Do thick fogs bother people where you live?	Yes	No
17.	Would a moth sting people?	Yes	No
18.	Is a thin string stronger than a thick one?	Yes	No
19.	Can you ring a gong with a hammer?	Yes	No
20.	Can you fling a rock with a sling shot?	Yes	No

UNIT 7

Spelling le Ending Words

Spell the *le* ending words. The first twelve have double consonants.

 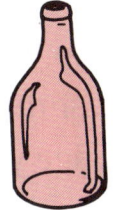 

1. _____ 2. _____ 3. _____

4. _____ 5. _____ 6. _____

  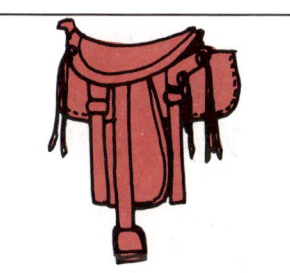

7. _____ 8. _____ 9. _____

 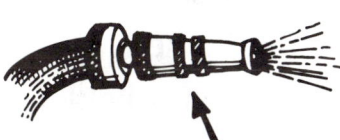 

10. _____ 11. _____ 12. _____

13. _____ 14. _____ 15. _____

UNIT 7

Reading Sentences

Read the sentences. Draw a line under **yes** or **no**.

1.	Do many people sink their putts on the golf links?	Yes	No
2.	Do you think a piece of cloth will shrink if it gets wet?	Yes	No
3.	Could you nibble on a piece of fudge you bought?	Yes	No
4.	Does a mink stink as badly as a skunk?	Yes	No
5.	Would you stumble on a little pebble?	Yes	No
6.	Must you think when you work on riddles and puzzles?	Yes	No
7.	Would a banker cash your blank check?	Yes	No
8.	Do nimble running backs dodge clumsy tackles?	Yes	No
9.	Do most catchers hit only singles?	Yes	No
10.	Can some left–handed pitchers toss sinkers?	Yes	No
11.	Could you build a bridge with a bundle of little planks?	Yes	No
12.	Do you think you can handle a simple math quiz at school?	Yes	No
13.	Would your friends laugh if you fumbled a simple pass?	Yes	No
14.	Would cattle have to struggle through a jungle?	Yes	No
15.	Do ping pong champs have to have paddles?	Yes	No
16.	Could your uncle trim a rough hedge with a sickle?	Yes	No
17.	Would a crippled tackle have to hobble to a huddle?	Yes	No
18.	Is it simple to settle other peoples' squabbles?	Yes	No
19.	Would a nozzle help you sprinkle a hedge?	Yes	No
20.	Should you sample pink punch from a bottle?	Yes	No

UNIT 8

Sounding Double-Vowel Words

When two vowel letters are together in a little word, sound the *name* of the first vowel and skip the second vowel. The silent second vowel letter tells you that the first vowel letter is long.

We spell /ā/ words with *ai* and *ay* as in

nai**l**   **tr**ay

We spell /ē/ words with *ee* and *ea* as in

whee**l**   **s**ea**l**
            (animal)

We spell /ī/ words with *ie* as in

tie
(neck)

We spell /ō/ words with *oa* and *oe* as in

boa**t**   **h**oe

We spell /ū/ words with *ue* and *ui* as in

blue   **s**ui**t**

UNIT 8

Sounding Double-Vowel Words

Say the letter sounds softly together to decode the words. Say the sight words.

> **SIGHT WORDS**
> kind sure climb shoe touch brought child group wind sign

rain	mail	coal	say	leak	way
bean	hay	team	oak	lay	soak
feet	aim	feed	cue	need	pay
seal	lean	deep	feel	laid	seen
kind*	deal	seed	foam	eat	leap
may	weak	sure*	lead	bait	sail
sea	climb*	main	meat	ray	beat
load	raid	bay	bead	died	shoe*
meat	clay	tail	weed	seat	week
green	trail	dream	toast	tried	feast
clay	free	spray	touch*	steal	speech
pray	waist	cheap	sheep	brought*	stay
paint	fleet	clean	least	plain	grain
child*	faint	brain	steep	braid	steel
gray	steam	group*	wheat	cheek	wind*
treat	stray	bleed	float	sprain	greet
strain	claim	play	cream	east	stream
pleat	sign*	plead	stain	speed	sheet
gleam	loan	greed	saint	scream	pain
suit	wait	fruit	dried	drain	fried

*Sight words

UNIT 8

Sounding Short and Long Vowel Words

Sound out the short and long vowel word pairs.

am—aim	red—read	maid—mad
bead—bed	paid—pad	met—meal
bat—bait	bet—beet	meet—met
bet—beat	feed—fed	lad—laid
lead—led	braid—brad	steep—step

net—neat	bleed—bled	cost—coast
mean—men	plain—plan	clam—claim
pal—pail	sped—speed	lied—lid
pan—pain	bran—brain	pet—peat
main—man	did—died	paint—pant

got—goat	aid—ad	soap—sop
ran—rain	wheat—whet	den—dean
set—seat	ten—teen	red—read
van—vain	cot—coat	skid—skied
beast—best	road—rod	pep—peep

be—bed	we—wet
so—sock	no—not
go—got	ho—hot
hi—hit	she—shed
me—met	lo—lot

45

UNIT 8

Reading Sentences

If the sentence is true, mark the **T**. If it is false, mark the **F**.

1. Sheep are very fond of feeding on green beans.   T   F
2. Putting a leash on a goat will surely keep it from straying.   T   F
3. A child does not need soap and water to wash and keep clean.   T   F
4. You could spray your boat with blue paint if you wished.   T   F
5. A play train will run only if you wind it.   T   F
6. A father and mother should read their child's mail.   T   F
7. A young oak tree needs the heat of the sun's kind rays.   T   F
8. You need at least three weeks to clean your teeth.   T   F
9. It is easy to strain your eyes with cheap glasses.   T   F
10. You may not put gray paint on a steel door.   T   F
11. Most teachers want to get plain talk from their groups of kids.   T   F
12. A pitcher should try to walk the other team's batters.   T   F
13. A young child will be fond of playing with clay.   T   F
14. Blue suits never get paint stains on them.   T   F
15. If you just touch your cheek with an oak leaf, it will bleed freely.   T   F
16. Neat people want to sleep on clean sheets.   T   F
17. Beets and oats are both grain crops.   T   F
18. People will feel weak if they do not eat cream of wheat.   T   F
19. We should give shoes, coats, and free meals to people who can't pay.   T   F
20. The last faint sun rays may have brought signs of rain.   T   F

UNIT 8

Spelling Double Vowel Words

Spell these nine long vowel /ā/ words with *ai*.

1. _____ 2. _____ 3. _____

4. _____ 5. _____ 6. _____

7. _____ 8. _____ 9. _____

Spell these three /ā/ words with *ay*.

1. _____ 2. _____ 3. _____

Add *ing* to these "doing" words.

4. _____ 5. _____ 6. _____

47

UNIT 8

Spelling Long Vowel Words

Spell these long vowel /ē/ words with *ee*.

1. _____ 2. _____ 3. _____

4. _____ 5. _____ 6. _____

7. _____ 8. _____ 9. _____

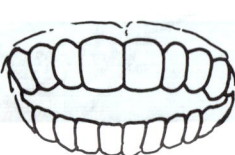  

10. _____ 11. _____ 12. _____

13. _____ 14. _____ 15. _____

UNIT 8

Spelling Double Vowel Words

Spell these /ē/ words with *ea*.

1. _____   2. _____   3. _____

  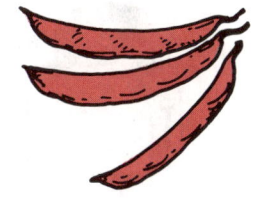

4. _____   5. _____   6. _____

7. _____   8. _____   9. _____

10. _____   11. _____   12. _____

What are they doing? Add *ing* to the verbs.

13. _____   14. _____   15. _____

49

UNIT 8

Spelling Double Vowel Words

Spell these /ō/ words with *oa*.

1. _____ 2. _____ 3. _____

4. _____ 5. _____ 6. _____

7. _____ 8. _____ 9. _____

10. _____ 11. _____ 12. _____

Spell these three /ō/ words with *oe*.

13. _____ 14. _____ 15. _____

50

UNIT 9

More Long Vowels

When a short word ends with *vowel-consonant-e*, sound the *name* of the vowel and skip the *e* sound. Say the letter sounds softly together to say the words. Do not stop between sounds.

Decode the words.

> **SIGHT WORDS**
> love ought though wear truth
> thought guess dead comb roll

make	bake	mule	tribe
ate	hope	safe	guess*
use	pile	bale	blade
roll*	cake	rice	skate
hike	rake	though*	flake
made	kite	mine	shine
cane	name	rope	shame
late	comb*	coke	globe
home	same	file	chose
poke	mole	pale	spade
take	lame	time	love*
cube	wear*	life	flame
bone	pole	bite	throne
mate	mile	ought*	trade
tide	wake	hide	these
truth*	dead*	shake	stake
lime	hate	grade	chime
bare	fame	stole	thought*
like	sale	grape	lane
fuse	line	hole	dame

*Sight words

UNIT 9

More Consonant Sounds

pl**ā**n**e**

Decode the words.

smile	crate
shone	frame
shape	stroke
white	dome
blame	smoke
state	slope
spoke	spike
stone	shade
spite	strike
stale	chase
bride	those
drape	plate
broke	choke
spine	plane
brake	whine
crate	spine
whale	stoke
crane	bribe
while	scrape
pride	glide

c spells /s/ before *e, i,* and *y*

cent   city   cycle

g spells /j/ before *e, i,* and *y*

gem   gin   gym

ace	age
face	cage
lace	page
pace	rage
race	sage
brace	wage
grace	stage
place	huge
trace	change
space	range
ice	grange
lice	hinge
mice	tinge
nice	singe
rice	lunge
price	plunge
slice	strange
spice	cringe
spruce	fringe
truce	sponge*

52

UNIT 9

Spelling Vowel-Consonant-e Words

Spell these vowel-consonant-*e* words.

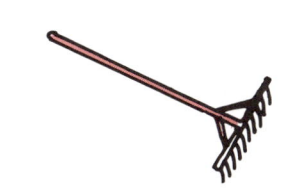  

1. _____ 2. _____ 3. _____

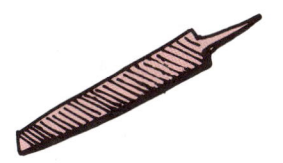  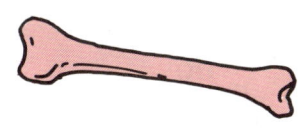

4. _____ 5. _____ 6. _____

7. _____ 8. _____ 9. _____

10. _____ 11. _____ 12. _____

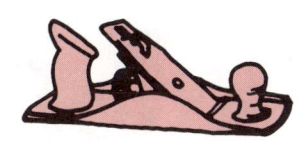  

13. _____ 14. _____ 15. _____

55

UNIT 10

Reading Stories

On the following pages are ten short stories for you to read to your teacher. The words in the stories are limited to short-vowel words, long-vowel words, and the 100 sight words listed below that you have learned in Units 2 through 9.

Read the stories silently and answer the questions so you will be able to read them orally to your teacher.

do	both	most	door	kind
of	would	what	father	sure
to	done	where	head	climb
who	any	live	wash	shoe
you	come	other	water	touch
does	none	watch	eye	brought
there	was	once	mother	child
have	put	very	talk	group
are	were	break	walk	wind
the	been	through	young	sign
buy	gone	front	piece	love
from	people	full	pull	ought
want	give	great	build	though
some	raid	taste	rough	wear
two	could	waste	laugh	truth
only	many	weigh	bread	thought
they	work	weight	here	guess
should	your	eight	shove	dead
move	their	change	bought	comb
one	friend	strange	school	roll

UNIT 10

1. The Fox and the Grapes

One hot summer day a fox was walking on the road thinking of nice things to eat. At last he spied some blue grapes hanging on a vine. The fox sat on the grass and smacked his lips. His eyes shone and his nose twitched.

"Mm—" he said. "I can just taste those grapes! They will make a nice meal. They are as plump and ripe as any I have seen this summer. See what a deep shade of blue they are! That means they are ripe and sweet. I am in luck!"

The fox smiled at the thought of such a treat. Slowly he backed off. He braced his hind legs and ran as swiftly as he could. Up he leaped, as high as he could.

"I just missed them by a few inches," he cried. "Next time I will reach them!"

He backed up a long way this time to get a longer space in which to run. He ran like a flash and jumped as high as he could. This time he missed the bunch of grapes by only six inches.

He landed on his back on the dusty road. He raised his head to see if he was being watched. Not a living thing was in sight. He lay on his side panting. After he had rested a while, he got up.

"I am a great jumper," he boasted, "and I will have those fine grapes. This time I will be sure to make it."

This time he ran a long way to get up speed. Up he sprang. This time he missed by three inches. He grew angry and leaped once, twice, three times, four times, five times. Each time he landed in the dust. But each time his leaps were weaker and weaker.

At last he got up. He gazed up at the grapes swaying gently in the wind. He raised his nose high and sniffed.

"Why am I wasting my time?" he cried. "Those grapes are not ripe yet! Who wants to eat green grapes? I am sure they would have made me sick."

If the sentence is true, mark **T**. If it is false, mark **F**.

1. The fox thought the grapes would make a nice meal.   T   F
2. The grapes were ripe and sweet.   T   F
3. The fox jumped only three times to get the grapes.   T   F
4. At last the fox said the grapes were not ripe.   T   F
5. The fox did not tell the truth.   T   F

2. The Wind and the Sun

"My friend Sun," said the Wind, "you are very strong. But you can see that I am much stronger. You are soft and gentle, but I am tough. When I go to work, I can rip pieces from buildings. I can make huge waves in the seas. Big trees can not stand when I blast them. It is plain to see that no one is so strong as I am. You may think that I am boasting, but tell me, pray, who can do such feats of great strength as I can?"

The Sun smiled gently.

"What you say is true, Wind," said the Sun. "But breaking things up and ripping things to pieces is not the only way to show strength."

"What other way is there?" cried the Wind. "Do you think you are as strong as I am? Let us have a real test of strength. I will show you that I can beat you any time."

"You still think you are stronger than I," said the Wind. "Think of some test, and we will see who is the better."

"Well," said the Sun, "do you see that man walking on that road on the coast? It is chilly where he is. He has on a big coat. Here is an easy test for a big strong brute such as you claim to be. Can you use your great strength to take his coat off? That should be easy."

The Wind laughed.

"What a silly test," he cried, "I can rip his coat to shreds. Just watch me!"

The Sun backed off while the Wind huffed and puffed. As the gusts got stronger, the man pulled his coat closer and closer to his body. The Wind raged and groaned and strained. The man bent his head and trudged on. A huge tree crashed in front of him blocking the road. Great waves came rolling in from the sea. The man clung to his coat and kept on going. At last the Wind had to give up.

"I can not make him do it, Sun,"" he said. "Let me see you try."

The Sun shone his hot rays on the man. When it was very hot, the man had to take his coat off. He packed it neatly and went on his way.

"Do you still think you are stronger than I," asked the Sun.

"You win, Sun," said the Wind meekly. "I guess I do boast a lot. There may be better ways of showing strength than to bully people."

Fill in the missing words.
1. The Wind said he was stronger than the _____.
2. The Wind wanted to have a test of _____.
3. The man was wearing a big _____.
4. The Wind could not make the _____ take off his _____.
5. The winner of the test was the _____.

3. The Frog and the Young Bug

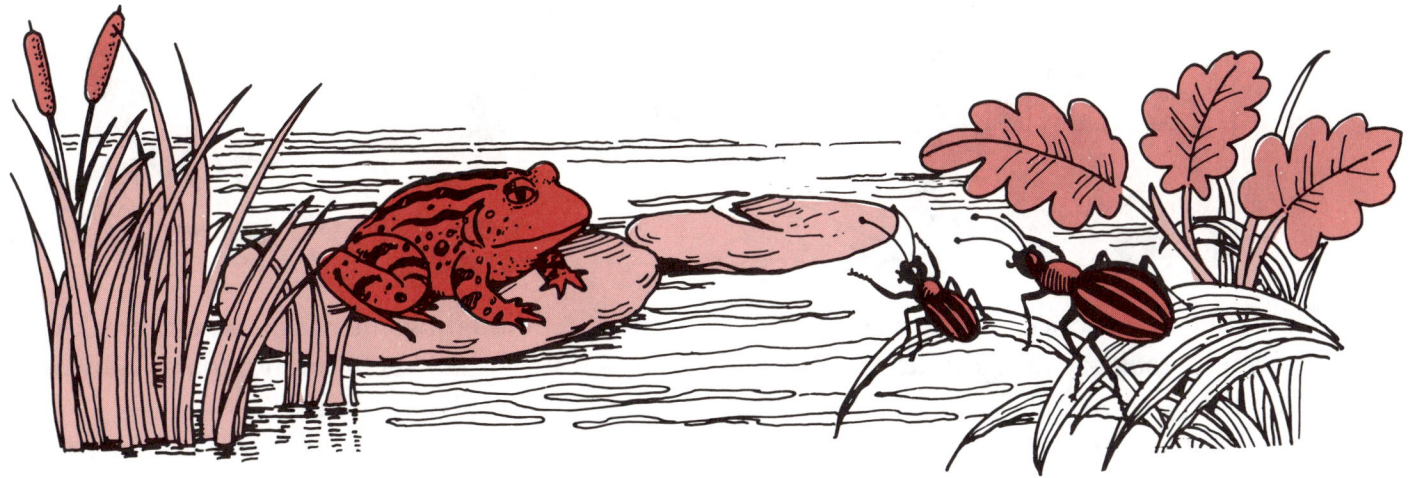

"Keep an eye on the frog, Son," said the mother bug to a brave young bug. "It is not safe to get close to that monster. He sits on that lily pad as if he were sleeping. I have seen lots of young bugs flit by that frog. He loves bugs and he will eat one after the other. That old frog has strong legs. He can leap at least ten feet!"

The young bug smiled. "Mother, you older bugs want to tell us young bugs what to do. You waste a lot of time talking, talking, talking. I am young, but I can fly like the wind. That sleepy old frog will never catch me."

The young bug made his way to the pond. There was the huge green frog sitting on his lily pad in the weeds.

"Silly frog!" laughed the vain young bug. "He is so big and fat that he can no longer move very fast. He will never touch me. I think I will play a game with him."

The young bug zipped past the frog, staying five or six feet from him. The fat frog did not move. Swish! The young bug flashed by, getting braver each time.

"I must try some of my dives," said the young bug. "That ought to make him move. I will try to get him to snap at me and slip off that lily pad and in the water. The water is like ice. That ought to wake him up!"

The young bug buzzed way up and then made a fast dive. Just as he got to the frog he changed speeds. There he hung, just an inch from the frog's nose.

Snap! And that was the end of the brave young bug. The frog smacked his lips and smiled.

"These young ones do think they are clever," he said. "Mother Bug, I hope you can teach your other young bugs better than you did this one."

Fill in the missing words.
1. The mother bug said the frog was a _____.
2. The frog liked to eat _____.
3. The mother bug said the frog had strong _____.
4. The young bug thought the frog could not _____ him.
5. The young bug thought he was very _____.

4. The Young Rat Plays a Trick

A big tribe of rats once lived in a shed. They were friendly rats—as rats go. The cats and dogs on the place would chase them from time to time, but they could not catch them. The older rats had seen that they could be safe if they helped each other. When the cats and the dogs got close to their shed, one rat would be sure to see them in time. The rat would then give three shrill squeaks and the other rats would head for their holes. That worked so well that the cats and dogs did not guess that so many rats lived in the shed.

But one day a young rat thought he would have some fun. While the other rats were playing games and feeding on the grain that was piled up in the bins, he quickly scampered by—and gave three shrill squeaks!

The rats sped past him and ran in their holes in a flash. Only one rat could be seen—the young rat who wanted to have fun. He rolled on the floor and held his sides as he laughed and laughed and laughed.

"Silly rats!" he cried. "It was only a trick. Come back. There is no cat here! My, you were funny! I thought some of you would break your legs. I never had such fun in my life. Why do you not come back, friends?"

Not one rat came. The young rat thought that was strange. He glanced in back of him. There was the CAT! A great big black cat came leaping at the young rat. He sprang to one side, just as the cat landed. He ran and ran as the big cat chased after him.

"Help! Save me!" cried the young rat. "Come and help me, friends!"

Just as he thought he was lost, he spied a crack that was just his size. He squeezed through and was safe at last. After the cat had left, the young rat crept from his hole. There sat his friends—the friends he had wanted to trick. They sat in a big ring and did not speak. The young rat hung his head in shame.

"Friends," he said. "I will never, never play that trick on you."

The young rat did keep his pledge. The rats in the shed are still safe from the cats and dogs. In fact, when one of them squeaks three times, you may be sure no rat can be seen.

Fill in the missing words.
1. One day a young rat planned to have some _____.
2. When the cat was not there, he gave three shrill _____.
3. When the rats ran to their holes, the young rat _____.
4. The young rat had to hang his _____ in _____.
5. The young rat will never play that _____ once more.

5. The Dog and the Cat

A young black and white dog and a big gray cat were pets in the same home. Each day, just as the sun set, they were fed their dinners. Their master placed two plates of chopped meat on the grass. The red plate had the dog's name painted on the side. The blue plate had the cat's name on it.

"Here is your meal, Shep," the master would say as he set the red plate on the grass. If the cat tried to eat from the red plate, the master would cry, "No! No!" He did the same thing with the cat's plate. If Shep got close to it, the master would chase him and cry, "No! No!" As long as the master kept an eye on the two, both got their meals and ate well.

But Shep did not like the cat, and the cat did not like Shep. If Shep was not there to get his meat, the cat would eat up his meat. If the cat was not there when the master fed them, Shep would eat the meat in both plates.

So the one that came late simply did not eat that day. The one that was there when the bowls were set out got sick from eating both meals. Both the cat and the dog were willing to scrap when they did not get a full meal. Shep would bite the cat and the cat would scratch Shep.

At last they were both so grumpy that they said they would stop their silly fussing.

"Cat," groaned Shep. "I ate your meat and I am sick. Last week you ate up my meat."

"Yes," said the cat, "and I was as sick as I could be. I did it just to be mean. I was not hungry."

"Let us sign a peace treaty," said Shep. "I give you my pledge that I will never touch the meat in your blue plate when you are not here."

"I will not rob your red plate if you will not rob mine. You eat only what is in your dish and I will eat only what is in mine," said the cat.

Both Shep and the cat did as they said they would. Both Shep and the cat got plenty to eat and they had their meals every day. Shep did not get sick any longer, and the cat did not get sick and did not go hungry. They both felt so well that they were fast friends. In fact, they play with each other to this very day and there are not two better friends in the land than Shep and the big gray cat.

Fill in the missing words.
1. The cat used to eat Shep's _____.
2. Shep used to eat the meat of the _____.
3. Shep ate so much he got _____.
4. The cat said she ate Shep's meat to be _____.
5. Shep said, "Let us sign a _____ _____."
6. Shep and the cat are fast _____.

6. The Fox and the Bees

A father fox was teaching his young one to hunt. The father fox was wise but the young fox was quite frisky and thought he was quite as clever as his father.

One day they came to a bee hive some miles from their cave. The young fox sniffed the sweet smell from the hive and he wanted to get to it.

"Watch it!" cried the old fox. "Those are bees. Bees sting. If those bees sting your tender young nose, you will feel pain—real pain."

The young fox sniffed the breeze and gazed at the hive. A few bees were buzzing as they came and went.

"Hm-m-m," said the young fox. "Quite a nice smell. Those things you say are bees are not big. They could not bother me, Father. I could jump up, dump the hive, and get us some of that sweet stuff."

"Quit making jokes," said the father fox. "Those bees are getting angry. It is time that we headed back to the cave. Come on!"

The father fox trotted off, thinking that the young fox would surely stick close to him. But the young fox did not do as he should. He crept close to the hive. He reached up and poked at it. An angry buzzing came from the hive.

"Buzz, buzz," laughed the young fox. "Bees of that size can not stop a brave young fox like me."

He slapped at the hive and tried to dump it. The angry bees came flying from the hive and went after the fox. At least twenty of the bees stung him. Never had he felt such pain!

The young fox raced off, slapping and brushing at the angry bees. At last he got free of them and crept back in the cave, licking the lumps from the bee stings.

"Well," said the wise father fox, trying to hide the grin on his face. "Some of us grow wise very slowly and we have to suffer pain in order to do so. What do you think of the bees? The bees are fine teachers, are they not?"

"I am a wiser fox than I was, Father," said the young fox softly. "I guess I will try better to do what you tell me. Did you ever get stung as I did?"

The father fox laughed. "Just twice," he said. "But I was not so wise as you are when I was young."

And what do you think? That young fox has been stung only once by bees in his life.

Fill in the missing words.
1. The father fox was teaching the young fox to _____.
2. The young fox thought he was as wise as his _____.
3. The young fox thought the _____ would not _____ him.
4. The angry bees _____ the young fox and gave him great _____.
5. The father fox said he had been stung _____ times.
6. The young fox got stung only _____.

7. The Silly Hen

"See those cute ducklings?" said Nell. "I love to see them swim in the pond."

"So do I," said Jane. "They make fine pets. I will feed them some grain."

Nell and Jane spent a great deal of time playing with the young ducks and feeding them. Each day they made a trip to the pond to see their pets. The ducklings would come running when they came to the pond.

A gray hen watched them day after day. She saw Nell and Jane feed the ducks and play with them.

"Why do they not feed me?" she cried. "I lay eggs, just as the ducks do. But no, they do not give me the time of day. I wish I were lucky and could be a duck. But, no, I am just a gray hen!"

The hen spent her days wishing she could be a duck. She got sadder and sadder, and thought she would rather be dead than be a hen. At last she spoke up.

"I will be a duck!" she cried. "I will act like a duck, and talk like a duck, and stay with ducks. I have the shape of a duck from my head to my tail! I am going to have fun as the ducks do. Then people will like me and pet me, and give me nice things to eat!"

The silly hen raced off to the pond to play with the ducks. She tried to quack like a duck, but she could only cluck like a hen. After a few days she was sure she was truly a duck.

"No one who sees me can tell that I am not a duck," she said. "I can walk like a duck. I can talk like a duck—cluck, cluck."

Then the mother duck lined up the young ducklings on the bank of the pond.

"Jump!" she cried. "It is time to swim. Cross the pond and swim back to me. Be brave, ducklings. It is easy to swim."

One by one the ducklings jumped in and swam. One by one they headed for the other side of the pond.

"I am a duck, so I can swim," thought the hen. "Now they will see that I am a true duck."

Splash!

The old hen dived in the pond—and under the icy water she sank!

"Help! Help!" she screamed. "My wings are soaked. I have water in my lungs! I see a big fish. It will bite me."

At last she got safely back on land. She was soaking wet. She ran off and hid till she was dry. She had a lot of time to think.

"What a silly thing I have been," she said at last. "I must be what I truly am—a hen."

The hen never wished to be a duck after that. She lived a long time and was quite happy the rest of a long life.

Fill in the missing words.
1. Nell and Jane liked to watch the _____ as they _____ in the _____.
2. Jane said she would feed the ducklings some _____.
3. The gray hen wanted to be a _____.
4. She said she would rather be _____ than be a _____.
5. The mother duck wanted the ducklings to _____ the _____ and _____ back.
6. The hen thought she could _____ in the _____, too.
7. When the hen dived in, she _____ under the icy _____.
8. She thought a _____ would bite her.
9. The silly hen got safely back on _____, but she was soaking.
10. At last she said that she had been very _____.

8. Spot and His Friend

It was Spot's job to keep the foxes from stealing Mrs. Jones' hens. Spot was a fine watchdog and did his job well, but he did get lonely. After the sun sunk the foxes came to steal a fat hen. Spot went after them and drove them from the place. Spot was big and strong, and he could run as fast as the foxes. At last, the foxes quit trying to get past the dog. But one sly fox thought he could get the better of Spot at his own game.

When Spot left the place, the sly fox stayed close to him. Spot got used to seeing the fox, so he did not chase after him. After three weeks the two got to be friends. Spot got quite fond of the fox. The sly fox would go closer and closer to Mrs. Jones' place when Spot had to get back home. Then he dropped in to see Spot after Mrs. Jones had gone to bed. At last the two got so friendly that where the fox went, you would see Spot. Spot was not lonely any longer.

When the sly fox thought it was time, he let the other foxes in on his plan to make a raid.

"Wait till I think the time has come," he said. "When I do, I will yelp three times. When I give you that sign, go after the hens. Mrs. Jones will be sleeping. Grab the hens and go. Spot will never get back in time. Then we will have a big feast in the cave on the hill."

Late that day the sly fox came to see his friend. Spot was glad to see him. He wagged his tail and ran to meet his friend.

"Let us trot to the pond, Spot," said the fox. "We can go hunting there and have some fun."

"But who will watch the hens?" asked Spot. "That is my job, old pal."

"Who would steal the hens?" asked the fox. "I am your friend. Have I tried to steal any hens?"

"Very well," said Spot. "I guess the hens will be safe."

When they got to the pond, the sly fox yelped three times.

"Why did you yelp?" asked Spot.

"I just felt like it," said the fox.

"What is that?" asked Spot. "The hens! The hens are screaming. They need help!"

Spot ran as fast as he could. The fox ran with him, staying close. When they came home, they could see the foxes running off. Each fox had a fat hen by the throat. Spot chased madly after the foxes. Just as he got close to one, the door slammed and Mrs. Jones came running with a gun. She raised it and aimed.

Crack!

Mrs. Jones missed the fox, but she hit Spot in the leg. Spot screamed with pain and rolled in the dust. Mrs. Jones came running. She could see the sly fox trot off grinning. She had watched Spot and his friend at play the past few weeks, so she guessed what the fox's plan had been.

"Do not blame me, Spot," she said. "If you run and play with bad friends, you will come to a bad end with them."

Spot has got used to being lonely, and he has never seen the sly fox—his fine friend. You may be sure he thinks twice when he picks his friends these days.

Fill in the missing words.
1. Spot's job was to keep the _____ from stealing the _____.
2. Spot did his job _____, but he did get _____.
3. The sly fox got to be Spot's _____.
4. The fox planned to make a _____ and catch some _____.
5. The fox said he would _____ three _____.
6. The fox wanted to have a big _____ in his _____ on the _____.
7. The fox said he would not _____ any _____.
8. Spot thought the hens would be _____.
9. Each of the fox's friends had a fat _____ by the _____.
10. Spot thinks _____ when he picks his _____ these days.

9. The Goats Raise a Crop

A group of goats lived on the side of a hill. They could see a man digging and planting seeds on the flat land at the end of the hill.

"See there," said one of the goats. "That man will reap crops of oats, wheat, beans, beets, and sweet peas. He will never need to hunt to get things to eat. At the end of the summer, he will gather his grain and sell some of it. The rest he will keep. When the rain and sleet come, he will have his grain to eat all winter long."

"Yes, that is true," said the next goat. "It is wise to plant crops. We should do the same. Then we could feast on the sweet tender grain when we want to. We will never have to munch on dry grass and weeds."

The other goats nodded their heads wisely. "Great plan!" they cried. "We want to help. We would love to get to work!"

The goats got some seeds. They dug deep holes and planted the seeds. Then they sat back and waited to see the green plants pop up. But there was no rain.

"We will have to get some pails and drag them up here from the stream," said one goat.

Some of the goats got to work dragging pails of water up to their crop land. The hot sun beat on their heads as they worked. Other goats lay in the shade under the trees and rested.

"I need some sleep," said one of the goats. "I think I will take a nap here in the shade."

She dropped off to dream of the feast that they would have when it was time to reap their crops. That left only six goats who were willing to work. Then one goat spoke up and said that he was feeling faint from the hot sun.

"I think I had better rest, friends," he said. "I feel very dizzy."

The five goats that were left worked a while longer. Then a goat spoke up and said, "Friends, I will have to quit a while. I do think I have twisted my left hind leg badly. The pain is killing me!"

The last four goats worked longer, digging up the weeds that had sprung up to choke their young plants. But then one of the four grunted as if he felt a pain.

"It is my throat!" he cried. "A bug must have bit me here on my neck. The pain is killing me. Help me! I will die if you do not help me."

Two of the goats helped him limp off to the shade under the tree. All three flopped on the grass and panted. The last goat watched them leave.

"I guess there is no use trying to raise a crop with no help," she said. And so she lay with the others and went to sleep.

That winter the rain and sleet did come. The grass dried up. The goats were lean and thin. They climbed up the hill trying to find some patches of green grass. They crept close to each other to keep from freezing.

"Friends," said one of the goats, "I have a great plan! Next spring we should get some seeds and plant a fine crop. We can reap the grain and keep it in a cave. We will have plenty to eat through the long winter. Are you willing to help?"

Each one of the goats nodded.

"Great plan!" they cried. "We will help. We love to work!"

Do you think the goats did reap a crop the next spring?

Fill in the missing words.

1. The goats could see that the man was _____ seeds.
2. The goat said that the man would reap crops of _____, _____, _____, _____, and _____ _____.
3. The goats got some _____, dug deep _____, and then _____ them.
4. When no rain came, the goats had to fill _____ of water from the _____ and drag them up the _____.
5. One by _____ the goats quit working and lay in the _____ to _____.
6. At last only one goat was left to do the _____.
7. That winter the goats had to _____ up the hill to spot some _____ of green _____.
8. They crept close to each other to keep from _____.
9. After the winter, the silly goats planned to get _____, plant a fine _____, and _____ the grain.
10. The goats said that they _____ to work.

UNIT 10

10. The Silly Milk Maid

The milk maid was not pleased with the job she had. She wanted to get rich and to do as she pleased.

"I work day after day," she thought, "and I do not get the kind of pay I should. I can not save up on my pay. What can I do?"

That day she got a lot of milk. She set a big pail to one side in back of the milk shed. She was sure they would not miss one pail of milk where she worked. When she was through working that day, she grabbed the pail of milk and left.

"Let me see," she said. "I will sell this pail of milk at one of the shops. They will be glad to pay me in cash. I will use the cash to buy some eggs—lots of eggs. And a hen. I will have the hen sit on the eggs. When the eggs hatch, I will get a lot of chicks. The chicks will get big. They will lay eggs—lots of eggs. Those eggs will hatch and will be chicks."

"Then I will wait till the price of hens goes up. I will sell the hens. That will bring in a lot of cash. I will be rich, rich, rich! I will buy some fine red and blue and green and white silk dresses. When I walk in the shops and on the streets, the men will watch me. "Will you be my wife?" they will cry. I will ask them if they are rich. If they are not, I will raise my chin and tell them to get lost. What fun that will be!"

"At last I will find a fine rich young man. I will let him beg me to wed a long time. At last I will say yes. I will live in a fine big home on a hill. I will have lots of people to work in my home, and cut the grass, and trim the trees. I will sleep as long as I wish. What fun that will be!"

"The king and the queen will ask me to come to dinner. The people will love me and bring me gifts. I will wear lovely rings and watches. I will. . . ."

Just then the milk maid tripped on a stone in the road. Splash! She fell flat in the dust. The milk spilled. Not one drop of milk was left!

Fill in the missing words.
1. The milk maid did not like the _____ she had.
2. She wanted to get _____ and do as she _____.
3. She thought she was not getting as much _____ as she should.
4. She set a big _____ of _____ in the back of the _____.
5. She planned to _____ the pail of _____ at one of the _____.
6. She planned to use the cash to buy lots of _____ and a _____ to sit on the eggs.
7. She wanted to buy some _____ and _____ and _____ dresses.
8. She hoped to wed a _____ young _____.
9. She hoped to live in a big _____ on a _____.
10. But the milk maid _____ on a _____ and _____ the milk.

Pupils Oral Reading Test

This is your oral reading test. Read it over silently so you will be able to read it orally to your teacher. Your teacher will make your test on the marking test form on pages 71–72 and enter the results of the test scores on page 73.

Snails and Slugs

Part 1

Any schoolchild loves tales of living things. I guess the snails ought to rank as one of the oddest. There are at least 80,000 kinds of them. They break up into three huge groups. There are the ones with lungs that live on dry land. There are many others that have gills and live only in the deep seas. Still others want to live under logs and stones close to fresh water, rivers, ponds, and hot springs. As a matter of fact, you could buy a little fresh water snail and have fun watching it in your fish tank at home.

Part 2

Some of the biggest snails may reach a length of two feet at the most, but none of them weigh very much. There are others, though, that may not get to be quite as big as a grain of rice. They have long, thin feelers and eyes in their heads as well as little biting teeth. Some feed on plants, and some on shreds of rotted fruit and pieces of dead flesh.

Snails have no legs with which to walk. They move quite well, though, through the use of a strong, supple disk. This disk has a gland that works like a tube of glue. The gland keeps squeezing bubbles of sticky juice in front of the gliding snail. The snail moves through the film of soapy slime as it if were sliding on the ice of a skating rink.

Snails go where they wish. They can climb up the steepest of ledges and roughest of ridges. Their thick disks never get badly cut and bruised. In fact, a snail could put its full weight on the very edge of a keen shaving blade and not suffer a scratch. You could do that kind of a stunt only if you were wearing some of those thick-soled shoes.

Part 3

Water snails have shells that are like winding rolls of clay. This shell is not only a nice place in which to hide from foes like ants and beetles. It is both a fine summer home and a winter lodge. You may be sure these snails do not ever have to seek strange shelters and build nests. They bring their homes with them when they move here and there. Should the rains quit a long time and a dry spell comes, the snail simply shoves its head into its shell at once and pulls its disk in at the other end. Then it shuts up shop, so to speak. That done, it seals its front and back doors with spit and gets settled to have a nice long nap. These snails may doze off as long as eight to nine weeks at a stretch. Were you to touch such a sleeping snail, you would not see a single sign of life. You would surely judge it dead and gone. But when the spring rains have come, you would see a quick change as the water washed and woke them back to life.

The gayly striped shells of some snails are thought to be real prizes. There are people who comb miles of beaches in hopes of spying one of these shells. The shells come in lovely shades and hues of pink, green, blue, and white.

Many people say that they love to eat snails. The simple tuth is that a snail does not have much taste. Snails are roasted in richly spiced butter that gives them their true taste. What would you think if your mother brought you toasted bread and a dish of snails as your lunch? Would that suit your taste? Would you laugh?

Part 4

Slugs are land snails. They have no shells, but some have a thin flat plate like a spine running through the middle of their backs. They have their eyes on one set of their two sets of feelers. None of the slugs mate. The slug is both father and mother to the young.

The great gray slug is a pest. It gobbles huge clumps of the richest grain plants and lays waste to the land. Costly sprays are grudgingly bought by the planters to kill off the slugs. If the struggle is lost and the worker gangs give up and do not quell the pests, the crop losses can be great.

If you do not act very lively and move quickly, your friends may talk and say you are a snail. People once said that a young man ought to be rude and rough and manly. They said he was made of snakes and snails and puppy dog tails, but that his cute sisters had been made of sweets and spice and other things nice.

Teacher's Test Marking Form

Your teacher will use this test marking form to record any errors you make as you read.

Snails and Slugs

Part 1

Any schoolchild loves tales of living things. I guess the snails ought to rank as one of the oddest. There are at least 80,000 kinds of them. They break up into three huge groups. There are the ones with lungs that live on dry land. There are many others that have gills and live only in the deep seas. Still others want to live under logs and stones close to fresh water, rivers, ponds, and hot springs. As a matter of fact, you could buy a little fresh water snail and have fun watching it in your fish tank at home.

Part 2

Some of the biggest snails may reach a length of two feet at the most, but none of them weigh very much as a rule. There are others, though, that may not get to be quite as big as a grain of rice. They have long, thin feelers and eyes in their heads as well as little biting teeth. Some feed on plants, and some on shreds of rotted fruit and pieces of dead flesh.

Snails have no legs with which to walk. They move quite well, though, through the use of a strong, supple disk. This disk has a gland that works like a tube of glue. The gland keeps squeezing bubbles of sticky juice in front of the gliding snail. The snail moves through the film of soapy slime as it if were sliding on the ice of a skating rink.

Snails go where they wish. They can climb up the steepest of ledges and roughest of ridges. Their thick disks never get badly cut and bruised. In fact, a snail could put its full weight on the very edge of a keen shaving blade and not suffer a scratch. You could do that kind of a stunt only if you were wearing some of those thick-soled shoes.

Part 3

Water snails have shells that are like winding rolls of clay. This shell is not only a nice place in which to hide from foes like ants and beetles. It is both a fine summer home and a winter lodge. You may be sure these snails do not ever have to seek strange shelters and build nests. They bring their homes with them when they move here and there. Should the rains quit a long time and a dry spell comes, the snail simply shoves its head into its shell at once and pulls its disk in at the other end. Then it shuts up shop, so to speak. That done, it seals its front and back doors with spit and gets settled to have a nice long nap. These snails may doze off as long as eight to nine weeks at a stretch. Were you to touch such a sleeping snail, you would not see a single sign of life. You would surely judge it dead and gone. But when the spring rains have come, you would see a quick change as the water washed and woke them back to life.

The gayly striped shells of some snails are thought to be real prizes. There are people who comb miles of beaches in hopes of spying one of these shells. The shells come in lovely shades and hues of pink, green, blue, and white.

Many people say that they love to eat snails. The simple truth is that a snail does not have much taste. Snails are roasted in richly spiced butter that gives them their true taste. What would you think if your mother brought you toasted bread and a dish of snails as your lunch? Would that suit your taste? Would you laugh?

Part 4

Slugs are land snails. They have no shells, but some have a thin flat plate like a spine running through the middle of their backs. They have their eyes on one set of their two sets of feelers. None of the slugs mate. The slug is both father and mother to the young.

The great gray slug is a pest. It gobbles huge clumps of the richest grain plants and lays waste to the land. Costly sprays are grudgingly bought by the planters to kill off the slugs. If the struggle is lost and the worker gangs give up and do not quell the pests, the crop losses can be great.

If you do not act very lively and move quickly, your friends may talk and say you are a snail. People once said that a young man ought to be rude and rough and manly. They said he was made of snakes and snails and puppy dog tails, but that his cute sisters had been made of sweets and spice and other things nice.

UNIT 10

Oral Test Scorecard

Name_____

Date_____

Test Item	Number	Errors

1. Sight Words   100   _____

2. Short Vowel Words   120   _____

3. Long Vowel Words   110   _____

   Long a (25) _____ Long e (30) _____ Long i (25) _____

   Long o (15) _____ Long u (15) _____

4. Two-Letter Consonants

   th (12) _____ sh (12) _____ (t)ch (10) _____ ng (10) _____

   wh (5) _____ nk (5) _____ dge (5) _____ qu (5) _____

5. Word Endings

   -s, es (85) _____ -d, ed (14) _____ -ing (15) _____

   -er (15) _____ -est (5) _____ -ly (12) _____ -le (12) _____

UNIT 11

Two-Letter Vowels

oo spells the vowel sound in **moon**. The dictionary shows the **moon** vowel like this: /ü/

oo also spells the vowel sound in **book**. The dictionary shows the **book** vowel sound like this: /ù/

tool	boost	goose		hook
droop	spool	loose		stood
roof	cool	noose		foot
shoot	toot	moose		crook
boot	boom	choose		took
root	loom	soothe		shook
zoo	noon	ooze		good
too	coop	groove		wool
stoop	food	stooge		hood
room	broom	snooze		look
roost	tooth	tooth		brook
smooth	pool	noose		wood
proof	loot	hoover		cook
stool	drool			hoof
troop	gloom			nook
soon	scoop			soot
loop	booth			cookie
fool	mood			

UNIT 11

Spelling /u̇/ and /ü/ Words

Spell these /u̇/ and /ü/ words.

  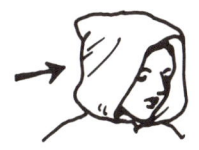

1. _____   2. _____   3. _____

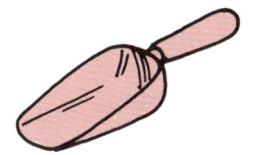  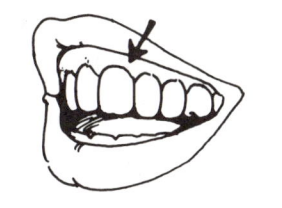

4. _____   5. _____   6. _____

7. _____   8. _____   9. _____

10. _____   11. _____   12. _____

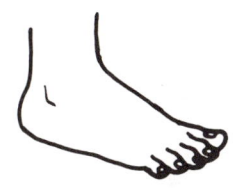  

13. _____   14. _____   15. _____

77

UNIT 11

Spelling ou, ow Words

ou spells the vowel sound in **house**.

ow spells the vowel sound in **cow**.

But **ow** also spells the **o** sound in **bow**.

stout	trout	plow	flow
round	crouch	gown	throw
sour	pout	clown	slow
our	sprout	frown	snow
out	bout	howl	blow
found	proud	now	own
south	ouch	down	show
ground	foul	town	grow
grouch	pouch	how	sow
pound	cloud	brown	low
shout	couch	owl	row
hound	loud	brow	glow
sound	flour	crown	crow
mouth	scout	drown	tow
mound	snout	growl	mow
blouse	ounce	prowl	bowl
house	bounce	fowl	stow
louse	pounce	vow	shown
rouse	trounce	bow	blown
	flounce	row	sown

78

UNIT 11

Spelling ou and ow Words

Spell these **ou** and **ow** words.

1. _____ 2. _____ 3. _____

4. _____ 5. _____ 6. _____

7. _____ 8. _____ 9. _____

10. _____ 11. _____ 12. _____

13. _____ 14. _____ 15. _____

UNIT 11

Spelling aw, au, a, oy, and oi Words

aw spells the vowel sound in **saw**

au also spells the vowel sound in **saw**

a before *l* also spells the vowel sound in **saw**

oy and **oi** spell the vowel sound in **boy**

aw	au	a	oy/oi
jaw	haul	all	boy
straw	fault	ball	joy
shawl	maul	call	toy
pawn	vault	fall	coy
draw	haunt	gall	boil
dawn	caulk	hall	coil
law	staunch	mall	soil
yawn	taunt	tall	spoil
lawn	paunch	wall	coin
brawl	launch	stall	join
hawk	flaunt	squall	point
thaw	jaunt	salt	joint
paw	aunt	malt	voice
raw	daunt	bald	choice
claw	gaunt	false	broil
crawl	daub	balk	foil
flaw	pause	talk	toil
drawl	clause	walk	moist
sprawl	cause	stalk	joist
brawn	sauce	chalk	hoist

UNIT 11

Spelling saw and boy Words

Spell these *saw* and *boy* words.

1. _____ 2. _____ 3. _____

4. _____ 5. _____ 6. _____

7. _____ 8. _____ 9. _____

10. _____ 11. _____ 12. _____

13. _____ 14. _____ 15. _____

UNIT 11

Word Meanings

If a pair of words has the same, or nearly the same meaning, mark **S**. If the words have opposite meanings, mark **O**.

1. smooth—rough   S O
2. cool—hot   S O
3. stoop—bend   S O
4. stood—sat   S O
5. pool—pond   S O
6. cook—bake   S O
7. glow—shine   S O
8. found—lost   S O
9. proud—humble   S O
10. shout—yell   S O
11. stool—seat   S O
12. throw—pitch   S O
13. low—high   S O
14. troop—group   S O
15. sooner—later   S O
16. boost—push   S O
17. loose—tight   S O
18. foot—head   S O
19. tooth—fang   S O
20. ooze—leak   S O
21. groove—rut   S O
22. took—gave   S O
23. good—bad   S O
24. stout—lean   S O
25. snooze—sleep   S O
26. sour—sweet   S O
27. brook—stream   S O
28. out—in   S O
29. pout—grin   S O
30. ground—soil   S O
31. loud—soft   S O
32. frown—smile   S O
33. tow—pull   S O
34. hoist—lift   S O
35. brawl—fight   S O
36. slow—fast   S O
37. all—none   S O
38. moist—dry   S O
39. pause—stop   S O
40. taunt—tease   S O

UNIT 11

Reading Sentences

1.	Should a boy scout be proud of doing a good deed?	Yes	No
2.	Would you like to hook a choice ten pound trout in a brook?	Yes	No
3.	Would a very tall moose have to stoop to get a cool drink at a pool in the woods?	Yes	No
4.	Can a batter be thrown out on a ground ball?	Yes	No
5.	Can a cook spoil his sauce with too much salt?	Yes	No
6.	Do people have to yawn when they grow drowsy?	Yes	No
7.	Would you frown and scowl if you saw the clowns do their stunts?	Yes	No
8.	Do people sit down on low stools when they milk cows?	Yes	No
9.	Would a hungry hawk soon swoop down on a fat fowl?	Yes	No
10.	Did you ever see a fawn pause on your front lawn at dawn?	Yes	No
11.	Are you ever in the mood to look at a good cookbook?	Yes	No
12.	Are there as many as twenty ounces in a pound of salt?	Yes	No
13.	Does the thought of clam chowder make your mouth drool?	Yes	No
14.	Should small boys throw chalk in school rooms?	Yes	No
15.	Would a cook scoop out flour with a small spoon?	Yes	No

UNIT 11

Reading Sentences

1. If you had a cat, could a small mouse run about loose in your house?   Yes   No
2. Do we need winter showers to make our spring flowers bloom?   Yes   No
3. Do school boys hate to throw snowballs?   Yes   No
4. Should we all talk with loud voices?   Yes   No
5. Is it true that hounds howl at the moon?   Yes   No
6. Will a rubber ball bounce off a stone wall?   Yes   No
7. Should you slow down when you drive through a strange town?   Yes   No
8. Does one need a good tool to saw wood?   Yes   No
9. Could a cowboy loop a noose around the neck of a cow?   Yes   No
10. Must a shop owner count out coins to make change?   Yes   No
11. Would the sound of loud shouts tend to soothe people?   Yes   No
12. Would a cook spoil the oysters by boiling them too long?   Yes   No
13. Does a batter walk if the pitcher balks?   Yes   No
14. Do the stalks of flowers grow brown in fall?   Yes   No
15. Do you get bawled out when they point out your faults?   Yes   No

UNIT 12

Vowel-R Sounds

ar spells the vowel-r sounds in ★
Dictionary spelling: /är/

er ur and **ir** spell the vowel-r sounds in **girl**
Dictionary spelling: /ėr/

yarn	wharf	her	sir	fur
march	farm	germ	thirst	curve
park	cart	nerve	flirt	curb
quart	tar	verb	first	burn
mark	arm	perch	birth	curl
part	sharp	jerk	stir	blur
art	card	stern	firm	church
darn	scar	serve	twirl	cur
car	far	fern	squirm	burst
spark	yard	clerk	chirp	hurt
warn	barn	herb	bird	purr
start	smart	herd	squirt	turn
chart	starch	term	third	spur
dark	charm	pert	whirl	surf
shark	war	swerve	dirt	hurl
lard	harp	berth	skirt	blurt
dart	bark	verse	shirt	nurse
scarf	warm	per	shirk	purse
warp	barb	perk	mirth	curse
bar	snarl	berg	girl	lurk
charge	large	merge	quirt	turf

Vowel-R Sounds

ear and **eer** spell the vowel-r sounds in **deer**
Dictionary spelling: /ir/

ear	deer
smear	cheer
fear	steer
clear	beer
spear	jeer
dear	peer
near	sheer
year	sneer
rear	leer
tear	queer
hear	veer

air and **are** spell the vowel-r sounds in **chair**
Dictionary spelling: /âr/

air	rare
hair	bare
chair	share
fair	snare
stair	care
pair	dare
dairy	spare
lair	stare
flair	scare
fairy	square
airy	hare

or and **ore** spell the vowel-r sounds in **fork**
Dictionary spelling: /or/

born	porch	shore
north	pork	stove
cord	fort	sore
torch	corn	ore
storm	thorn	core
cork	stork	chore
form	horn	bore
for	sport	tore
torn	short	store
scorch	sort	score

UNIT 12

Word Meanings

If a pair of words has the same, or nearly the same meaning, mark **S**. If the words have opposite meanings, mark **O**.

1. rear—front S O
2. fair—foul S O
3. darn—mend S O
4. warp—bend S O
5. barb—hook S O
6. square—round S O
7. squirt—spray S O
8. short—long S O
9. burn—scorch S O
10. cure—heal S O
11. burst—break S O
12. hurl—throw S O
13. her—him S O
14. dirt—soil S O
15. park—drive S O
16. snare—trap S O
17. start—stop S O
18. snarl—growl S O
19. sharp—dull S O
20. cheer—yell S O
21. jerk—pull S O
22. far—near S O
23. herd—swarm S O
24. war—peace S O
25. reverse—turn S O
26. stir—mix S O
27. large—small S O
28. twirl—spin S O
29. verb—noun S O
30. spare—save S O
31. first—last S O
32. curve—bend S O
33. clear—dim S O
34. torn—ripped S O
35. sort—kind S O
36. north—south S O
37. chore—work S O
38. girl—boy S O
39. lard—fat S O
40. smart—clever S O

UNIT 12

Reading Sentences

Draw a line under **Yes** or **No**.

1.	Could a clerk in a store charge too much for a shirt?	Yes	No
2.	Could a girl buy a purse to match her skirt?	Yes	No
3.	If a hurler's arm hurts, should he be throwing curves?	Yes	No
4.	Would you use a large barn on a dairy farm?	Yes	No
5.	Can a smart driver steer a car on a sharp curve?	Yes	No
6.	Can a bird eat a large ear of corn in a short time?	Yes	No
7.	Can runners score from both first and third on a fly ball?	Yes	No
8.	Would a loud thunder storm scare a herd of deer?	Yes	No
9.	Can you use *squirt* and *squirm* as verbs?	Yes	No
10.	Can you make a torch burn for nearly a year?	Yes	No
11.	Would a quart of root beer quench one's thirst?	Yes	No
12.	Do people park their cars near the curb?	Yes	No
13.	Does a girl need a lot of nerve to curl her hair?	Yes	No
14.	Do some parts of fairy tales still scare you?	Yes	No
15.	Would you hear cheers for the marching bands?	Yes	No

UNIT 12

Spelling ar Words

Spell the ar words.

1. _____

2. _____

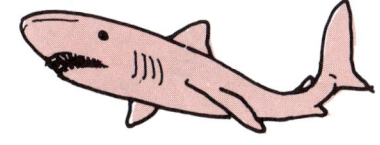
3. _____

4. _____

5. _____

6. _____

7. _____

8. _____

9. _____

10. _____

11. _____

12. _____

13. _____

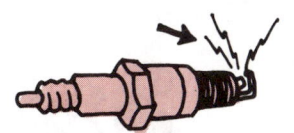
14. _____

15. _____

UNIT 12

Spelling er, ir and ur Words

Spell these er, ir, and ur words.

1. _____   2. _____   3. _____

4. _____   5. _____   6. _____

7. _____   8. _____   9. _____

 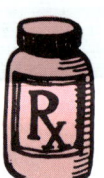 

10. _____   11. _____   12. _____

13. _____   14. _____   15. _____

UNIT 12
Spelling ear, eer, air, are, or, and ore Words

Spell the **ear**, **eer**, **air**, **or** and **ore** words.

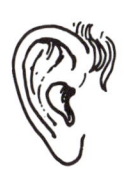  

1. _____   2. _____   3. _____

  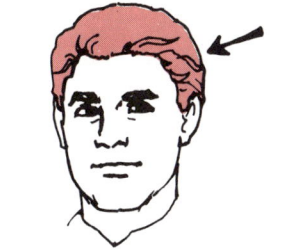

4. _____   5. _____   6. _____

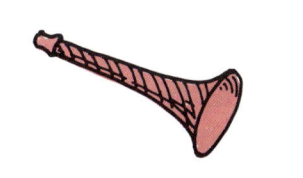  

7. _____   8. _____   9. _____

10. _____   11. _____   12. _____

13. _____   14. _____   15. _____

91

Vowel-R Endings

The vowel sounds in the **ar**, **er**, and **or** word endings are soft vowel sounds. The endings are sounded the same in—

burglAR   barbER   sailOR

Dictionary spelling: /ər/

Sound out these /ər/ words.

ar	er	or
beggar	silver	actor
hangar	whisker	tractor
dollar	ladder	tailor
collar	teacher	color
cellar	hammer	mayor
altar	shower	pastor
pillar	locker	author
polar	flower	doctor
cedar	zipper	motor
molar	fender	razor
mortar	drawer	mirror
grammar	speller	sponsor

UNIT 12

Spelling Vowel-R Ending Words

Spell these three **ar** ending words.

 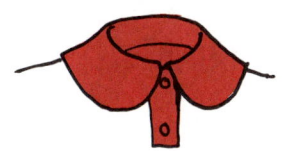 

1. _____   2. _____   3. _____

Spell these three *or* ending words.

4. _____   5. _____   6. _____

Spell these six *er* ending words.

7. _____   8. _____   9. _____

  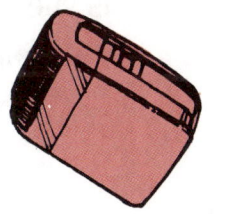

10. _____   11. _____   12. _____

Silent Consonants

Some words have consonant letters that do not spell sounds. They are silent letters.

The Tricky *gh* Words

GH is silent in the **high** and **right** groups, but the *i* before *gh* spells /ī/ instead of /i/.

high	right	might	plight
nigh	night	tight	bright
sigh	fight	sight	flight
thigh	light	slight	fright

GH is silent in the **aught** group. The *au* spells /ô/, as it should.

aught	daughter	naughty
naught	slaughter	haughty
caught		
taught		

GH is silent in the **ought** group, but *ou* spells /o/ instead of /ou/, as it should.

ought	bought	sought
fought	brought	thought

GH is silent in these words, but this *ou* may or may not spell /ou/.

bough /bou/   dough /dō/
plough /plou/   though /thō/

GH is silent in these words, but the *ei* spells /ā/.

sleigh	eight	straight /strāt/
neigh	freight	But:
weigh	weight	height /hīt/

And **GH** spells /f/ in these sight words.

rough /ruf/   cough /kôf/
tough /tuf/   enough /inuf′/
laugh /laf/   trough /trôf/

UNIT 13

Silent Consonants

The **k** is silent before *n* in words like these.

knock	*knob*	*knight*	*knuckle*
know	*knot*	*knack*	*knickers*
knife	*knit*	*knead*	*knell*
knee	*kneel*	*knave*	*knoll*

The **w** is silent before *r* in words like these.

wrap	wrist	wren	wry
wreck	write	wreath	wrestle
wring	wrote	wrath	wriggle
wrung	wrench	wretch	wrinkle

The final **b** is silent after *m* in words like these.

bomb	dumb	climb /klīm/
crumb	thumb	comb /kōm/
limb	lamb	
numb	jamb	

But **b** is *not* silent after *m* in *er* and *le* words like these.

lumber	limber	scramble	tremble
timber	slumber	tumble	stumble
number	ember	thimble	humble
member	amber	mumble	grumble

The **t** is silent before *le* in words like these.

castle	gristle	thistle
trestle	jostle	whistle
bristle	rustle	wrestle

The **l** is silent in words like these.

calm	half	walk
palm	calf	chalk
balm	halves	stalk
qualm	calves	balk

UNIT 13

Word Meanings

If a pair of words has the same, or nearly the same meaning, mark **S**. If the words have opposite meanings, mark **O**.

		S	O			S	O
1.	high—low	S	O	21.	knit—weave	S	O
2.	thigh—leg	S	O	22.	tight—loose	S	O
3.	haughty—proud	S	O	23.	fright—scare	S	O
4.	bough—limb	S	O	24.	bought—sold	S	O
5.	bright—dull	S	O	25.	sleigh—sled	S	O
6.	naughty—good	S	O	26.	slight—little	S	O
7.	ought—should	S	O	27.	knock—tap	S	O
8.	height—weight	S	O	28.	nigh—far	S	O
9.	wring—twist	S	O	29.	wrap—fold	S	O
10.	wrath—anger	S	O	30.	limber—nimble	S	O
11.	rough—smooth	S	O	31.	tremble—shiver	S	O
12.	wriggle—squirm	S	O	32.	right—wrong	S	O
13.	tough—hard	S	O	33.	mumble—grumble	S	O
14.	laugh—cry	S	O	34.	straight—crooked	S	O
15.	lumber—timber	S	O	35.	left—right	S	O
16.	lamp—sheep	S	O	36.	slumber—sleep	S	O
17.	jostle—push	S	O	37.	day—night	S	O
18.	dumb—smart	S	O	38.	light—dark	S	O
19.	thistle—thorn	S	O	39.	brought—sent	S	O
20.	knack—skill	S	O	40.	haughty—humble	S	O

UNIT 13

Reading Sentences

Draw a line under **Yes** or **No**.

1.	Does one use his wrist to twist a wrench to the right?	Yes	No
2.	If she were taught what is right, might a naughty daughter listen to her mother?	Yes	No
3.	Is it wrong for butchers to lead lambs and calves to slaughter?	Yes	No
4.	Would you need a bright light to tie a knot at night?	Yes	No
5.	Did good knights once fight to right wrongs?	Yes	No
6.	Ought one kneel to turn the knob on a door?	Yes	No
7.	Must you use your thumb to write with chalk?	Yes	No
8.	Was it once thought wrong for knights to fight with knives and daggers?	Yes	No
9.	Would the sight of a car wreck make you tremble with fright?	Yes	No
10.	Does a dumb beast know right from wrong?	Yes	No
11.	Would a catcher often jamb his thumb?	Yes	No
12.	Do bright young kids often listen to their mothers and fathers calmly?	Yes	No
13.	Do planes climb very high in making their flights?	Yes	No
14.	Does the palm of your hand grow numb when you write?	Yes	No
15.	Could you train a smart lamb to come when you whistle?	Yes	No

UNIT 13

Spelling Silent Consonant Words

Spell these silent consonant words.

1. _____

2. _____

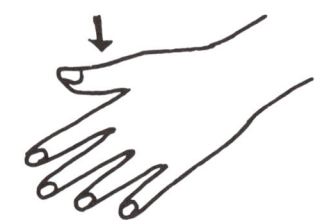

3. _____

4. _____

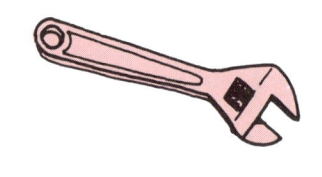

5. _____

6. _____

7. _____

8. _____

9. _____

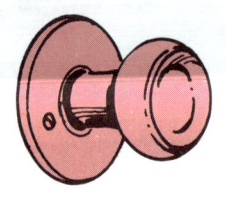

10. _____

11. _____

12. _____

13. _____

14. _____

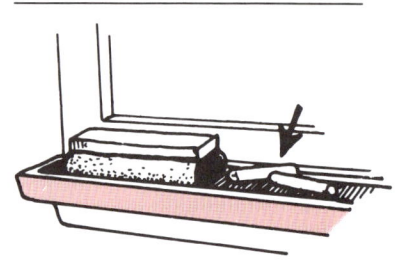

15. _____

98

Pupils Oral Reading Test

This is your oral reading test. Read it over silently so you will be able to read it orally to your teacher. Your teacher will mark your test on the marking test form on pages 113–116 and enter the results of the test scorecard on page 117.

Birds

Part 1

People who love and care for birds dearly have been watching them for many years. We call them bird watchers. Would you have guessed that there are more than 9000 sorts or kinds of birds? There are a great many more land birds than water birds. Both the smaller and larger ones are in the land group. Perching birds like finches, crows, larks, wrens, starlings, and so forth, roost on tree branches. Water birds choose to live fairly close to the shores of fresh water ponds, lakes, and brooks.

Most bird pairs build nests in which the mothers lay eggs and shelter their young when the chilling winds blow and the rain and snow storms come. Some nesters dig holes in the trunks of tall dead trees. Marsh birds like the grebes build their houses on floating rafts that they make from spoiled and rotted plants. They moor them to reefs and weed stalks. Swifts build saucer-shaped nests in the tree crotches so their eggs will not be seen by high flying birds. Some nests are just strange looking pouches hanging from the boughs of trees.

All birds are born from eggs hatched by the warmth of the mother's body. It is said that very large birds lay only one, or, rarely, two eggs a year. Some smaller ones lay a great many more, often as many as twenty at a time. A duck could lay 350 or more eggs in a year.

The young birds have to break through their shells in order to hatch. Once they crawl out, they chirp and squawk noisily. They twitch their little wings eagerly. Soon they want to be gone to start their first air flight. They dare to shove off and often fly as far as 100 yards while the mother watches proudly.

Part 2

Young, quickly growing birds have to be fed daily by the father and mother birds. Some young birds eat nearly their own weight in food on a single day. Most small birds eat any kind of seeds, pieces of fruit, bread crumbs, bugs, and grubs.

Birds eat weed seeds and thus help farmers keep their plowed land free of weeds. They gobble up the pests that can nearly drive the poor farmers up the wall. It was once noted that birds ate more than 300 weed seeds per square foot of farm soil in one year. Hawks and owls help by swooping down from a tree limb or barn roof and pouncing on mice and rats.

Some foolish farmers shoot at the soaring hawks in fear that they would kill and feed on their farm fowl. None of the farmers ought to do that, though, for those birds do far more good than the harm done to the farmers. The plain truth is that birds were and are the farmers' friends. They should be known as yours, too, no matter what you do or where you live. Those rash farmers can surely spare the ears of corn the birds take. In fact, smart farmers use their heads and do put out food for the birds.

Birds bring much joy to watchers on their bird walks by singing their songs of good cheer. The wood thrush has the most charming of all the tunes people love to hear.

Birds use their shrill voices to warn others when a foe is drawing too near. Quails utter a so-called gathering call. It causes the scared birds to scatter for shelter. The crows caw and the owls hoot to give warning signs to their friends to move in a hurry. Even the mute, dumb storks, who have no voices at all, make loud clacking sounds with their huge bills. Some birds can be taught to talk. Some cackle and whistle as if they were laughing at us.

Part 3

Any schoolchild can see that birds do not all have the same kind of feet. Some water birds have wading feet so they can prowl the pools and puddles to scout for food. Ducks and loons have webbed feet to paddle through water. Other birds have sharp curved claws to climb and clutch the rough bark of trees. Perching birds have three jointed toes that point to the front and one that points to the rear. That helps them clamp their toes on smooth, round, tree branches.

Nor do all birds have the same kinds of beaks. The finches need short cracker beaks with the power to crush the hard shells of the seeds they eat. Some water birds have needle-like bills shaped like spears to jab at fish. The brown creepers have long, slender bills that work like tweezers. Others have bills shaped like spoons to scoop in small fish and water bugs. Still others have strainer beaks which have fine combs to screen out the mud they must wash from the plant sprouts they pull out of the water.

Part 4

You can help the birds in spring by furnishing them with the things they need to build their nests. Lay out some short pieces of string and yarn, some straw, and some scraps of waste and cloth.

Birds get thirsty, too, and they like to splash and bathe in clear, cool water. Putting up a bird bath will bring the birds flocking to your front lawn or back yard.

Birds need our help in winter. Start putting down food in the late fall. Keep putting it in the same place, where it is easily found. Set the food out after dark so the birds will see it first thing at the crack of dawn. Rendered beef fat can be bought cheaply at the stores. Buy eight or ten strips. Climb a tree and hang it on a stout string or cord. Do that so your naughty cat does not share this choice bird fare. If you can't buy the beef fat, mix some bird seed in lard. Stuff it in a mesh sack and hang it from a tree branch.

You can serve the birds chopped up hard–boiled eggs, nuts, seeds, rolled oats, raw rice, crumbled bread, fruit, and cooked fish. Smear some peanut butter on crackers. Birds love the taste.

Make the birds a feeding shelf. Use a square board a foot in length and width. Tack on a roof to ward out sleet and snow. Bore holes in the corners so the water will run off freely. Nail the shelf up near your back door. There you can sprawl on your easy chair and keep an eye on your bird friends. You will soon be pleased that you thought of serving brunch to your winged friends. Do join the bird watchers!

Teacher's Test Marking Form

Your teacher will use this test marking form
to record any errors you make as you read.

Birds

Part 1

People who love and care for birds dearly have been watching them for many years. We call them bird watchers. Would you have guessed that there are more than 9000 sorts or kinds of birds? There are a great many more land birds than water birds. Both the smaller and larger ones are in the land group. Perching birds like finches, crows, larks, wrens, starlings, and so forth, roost on tree branches. Water birds choose to live fairly close to the shores of fresh water ponds, lakes, and brooks.

Most bird pairs build nests in which the mothers lay eggs and shelter their young when the chilling winds blow and the rain and snow storms come. Some nesters dig holes in the trunks of tall dead trees. Marsh birds like the grebes build their houses on floating rafts that they make from spoiled and rotted plants. They moor them to reefs and weed stalks. Swifts build saucer-shaped nests in the tree crotches so their eggs will not be seen by high flying birds. Some nests are just strange looking pouches hanging from the boughs of trees.

All birds are born from eggs hatched by the warmth of the mother's body. It is said that very large birds lay only one, or, rarely, two eggs a year. Some smaller ones lay a great many more, often as many as twenty at a time. A duck could lay 350 or more eggs in a year.

The young birds have to break through their shells in order to hatch. Once they crawl out, they chirp and squawk noisily. They twitch their little wings eagerly. Soon they want to be gone to start their first air flight. They dare to shove off and often fly as far as 100 yards while the mother watches proudly.

Part 2

Young, quickly growing birds have to be fed daily by the father and mother birds. Some young birds eat nearly their own weight in food on a single day. Most small birds eat any kind of seeds, pieces of fruit, bread crumbs, bugs, and grubs.

Birds eat weed seeds and thus help farmers keep their plowed land free of weeds. They gobble up the pests that can nearly drive the poor farmers up the wall. It was once noted that birds ate more than 300 weed seeds per square foot of farm soil in one year. Hawks and owls help by swooping down from a tree limb or barn roof and pouncing on mice and rats.

Some foolish farmers shoot at the soaring hawks in fear that they would kill and feed on their farm fowl. None of the farmers ought to do that, though, for those birds do far more good than the harm done to the farmers. The plain truth is that birds were and are the farmers' friends. They should be known as yours, too, no matter what you do or where you live. Those rash farmers can surely spare the ears of corn the birds take. In fact, smart farmers use their heads and do put out food for the birds.

Birds bring much joy to watchers on their bird walks by singing their songs of good cheer. The wood thrush has the most charming of all the tunes people love to hear.

Birds use their shrill voices to warn others when a foe is drawing too near. Quails utter a so-called gathering call. It causes the scared birds to scatter for shelter. The crows caw and the owls hoot to give warning signs to their friends to move in a hurry. Even the mute, dumb storks, who have no voices at all, make loud clacking sounds with their huge bills. Some birds can be taught to talk. Some cackle and whistle as if they were laughing at us.

Part 3

Any schoolchild can see that birds do not all have the same kind of feet. Some water birds have wading feet so they can prowl the pools and puddles to scout for food. Ducks and loons have webbed feet to paddle through water. Other birds have sharp curved claws to climb and clutch the rough bark of trees. Perching birds have three jointed toes that point to the front and one that points to the rear. That helps them clamp their toes on smooth, round, tree branches.

Nor do all birds have the same kinds of beaks. The finches need short cracker beaks with the power to crush the hard shells of the seeds they eat. Some water birds have needle-like bills shaped like spears to jab at fish. The brown creepers have long, slender bills that work like tweezers. Others have bills shaped like spoons to scoop in small fish and water bugs. Still others have strainer beaks which have fine combs to screen out the mud they must wash from the plant sprouts they pull out of the water.

Part 4

You can help the birds in spring by furnishing them with the things they need to build their nests. Lay out some short pieces of string and yarn, some straw, and some scraps of waste and cloth.

Birds get thirsty, too, and they like to splash and bathe in clear, cool water. Putting up a bird bath will bring the birds flocking to your front lawn or back yard.

Birds need our help in winter. Start putting down food in the late fall. Keep putting it in the same place, where it is easily found. Set the food out after dark so the birds will see it first thing at the crack of dawn. Rendered beef fat can be bought cheaply at the stores. Buy eight or ten strips. Climb a tree and hang it on a stout string or cord. Do that so your naughty cat does not share this choice bird fare. If you can't buy the beef fat, mix some bird seed in lard. Stuff it in a mesh sack and hang it from a tree branch.

You can serve the birds chopped up hard–boiled eggs, nuts, seeds, rolled oats, raw rice, crumbled bread, fruit, and cooked fish. Smear some peanut butter on crackers. Birds love the taste.

Make the birds a feeding shelf. Use a square board a foot in length and width. Tack on a roof to ward out sleet and snow. Bore holes in the corners so the water will run off freely. Nail the shelf up near your back door. There you can sprawl on your easy chair and keep an eye on your bird friends. You will soon be pleased that you thought of serving brunch to your winged friends. Do join the bird watchers!

Oral Test Scorecard

Name _____

Date _____

<u>Test Item</u>   <u>Number</u>   <u>Errors</u>

1. Sight Words   95 _____

2. Short Vowel Words   115 _____

3. Long Vowel Words

4. Two-Letter Vowel Words   80 _____

            ou
   oo (26) _____ ow (25) _____

   aw   oi
   au (21) _____ oy (9) _____
   al

5. Vowel-*r* Words

           er
   ar (20) _____ ir (10) _____
           ur

   ear   air
   eer (12) _____ are (12) _____

   or
   ore
   oar (20) _____

6. Two-Letter Consonants   85 _____

   th (25) _____ sh (20) _____ (t)ch (20) _____

   ng (10) _____ uh (5) _____ qu (5) _____

7. Word Endings   180 _____

   s, es (75) _____ d, ed (20) _____

   -ing (25) _____ er (30) _____

   -ly (15) _____ qu (5) _____

   le (10) _____

Compound Words

We make compound words by putting shorter words together. The word parts of these compounds have the same short-vowel, long-vowel, two-vowel, and vowel-r spellings that you have been decoding since Unit 1. Compounds also have the sight word and silent-letter spellings.

Draw lines between the word parts and decode the words.

Compounds with the short-vowel word parts

upset	eggshell
handbag	grasshopper
backhand	gangplank
catfish	shotgun
sandbox	snapshot
himself	pigpen
windmill	quicksand
bathtub	lumberjack
grandstand	potluck
stickpin	quicksand
kickoff	sandman
fisherman	slapstick
skullcap	bandstand
shellfish	hubcap
handspring	sunfish
indent	handcuff
understand	shiftless
offset	drumstick
uphill	membership
slipshod	

Compounds with the long-vowel word parts

streamline	sailboat
oatmeal	grapefruit
fireplace	railroad
fireside	maybe
seacoast	driveway
rainbow	teammate
steamboat	pipeline
daytime	playmate
lifeboat	seaplane
daydream	suitcase
homemade	lifetime
goalkeeper	rowboat
nosebleed	mainstream
raincoat	bluejeans
slowpoke	snowflake
limeade	piledriver
lifelike	flywheel
drainpipe	pieplate
coastline	skyline
seaside	bluejay

UNIT 15

Spelling Short-Vowel Compounds

Spell the short-vowel compounds.

1. _____ 2. _____ 3. _____

4. _____ 5. _____ 6. _____

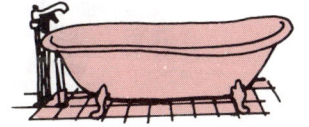  

7. _____ 8. _____ 9. _____

 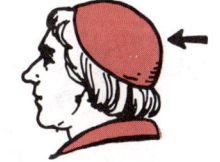 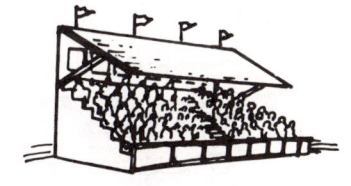

10. _____ 11. _____ 12. _____

123

UNIT 15

Spelling Long-Vowel Compounds

Spell the long-vowel compounds.

1. _____

2. _____

3. _____

4. _____

5. _____

6. _____

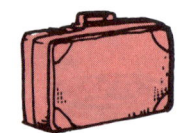
7. _____

8. _____

9. _____

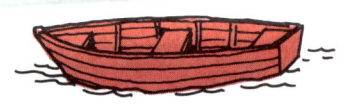
10. _____

11. _____

12. _____

UNIT 15

Compound Words

Compounds with short and long word parts

Compounds with two-vowel word parts

Compounds with two-vowel and short vowel parts

Draw lines between the word parts and decode the words.

underline	rosebud	roundhouse	bookcase	bedroom
blueprint	mailman	outlaw	snowball	background
haystack	classmate	foolproof	greenhouse	bathroom
brakeman	necktie	lookout	notebook	toothbrush
peanut	inside	footstool	playground	fishhook
pancake	nobody	outlook	fireproof	woodpecker
butterfly	mailbox	downtown	housewife	textbook
fireman	upkeep	football	playroom	checkbook
hopeless	lifeless	cowboy	toadstool	saucepan
offside	backbone	outbound	proofread	broomstick
spineless	handmade	soundproof	teaspoon	crawfish
bedside	steamship	poorboy	bookkeeper	jigsaw
runway	sealskin	shootout	blowout	sawdust
salesman	wishbone	bloodhound	tryout	oilcloth
cupcake	bedtime	loudmouth	downstream	classroom
bathrobe	sunshine	boyhood	sunflower	downhill
raindrop	flagpole	cookbook	hallway	pinpoint
hitchhike	sheepskin	downpour	looseleaf	footprint
bedsheet	teapot	outshoot	woodpile	withdraw
fusebox	doeskin	falsehood	soybean	jawbone

UNIT 15

Spelling Short-Long Vowel Compounds

Spell the short and long vowel compounds.

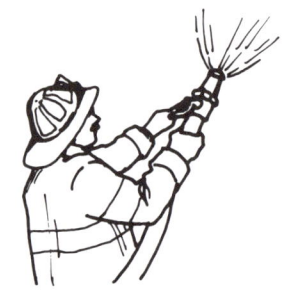

1. _____   2. _____   3. _____

4. _____   5. _____   6. _____

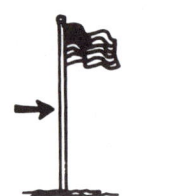

7. _____   8. _____   9. _____

10. _____   11. _____   12. _____

UNIT 15
Spelling Compounds with Two-Vowel Parts

Some of these compounds combine two-vowel parts with long and short vowel parts. Write the spellings.

1. _____   2. _____   3. _____

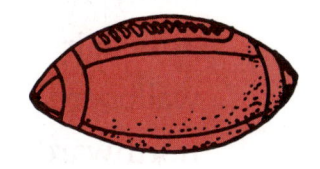

4. _____   5. _____   6. _____

7. _____   8. _____   9. _____

10. _____   11. _____   12. _____

127

UNIT 15

Compound Words

Compounds with Vowel-R Parts

Compounds with Vowel-R and Short Vowel Parts

Compounds with Vowel-R and Long Vowel Parts

Draw lines between the word parts and decode the words.

airport	upstairs	horseback	bluebird
cardboard	shortstop	quarterback	streetcar
forearm	popcorn	boxcar	airplane
farmyard	fearless	uproar	foresee
armchair	foretell	harmless	eastward
wallboard	upward	offshore	northeast
northward	upturn	northwest	seaport
chalkboard	eardrum	onward	stairway
yardarm	haircut	passport	turnpike
airborne	forecast	careless	trademark
surfboard	blackbird	billboard	cornmeal
forewarn	warship	yardstick	blowtorch
shorthorn	springboard	shipyard	rainstorm
hardware	pitchfork	shorthand	cheeseburger
carport	hamburger	limburger	crowbar
carfare	sparkplug	catbird	carefree
careworn	herself	windstorm	porthole
churchyard	sparerib	sportsman	hailstorm
forlorn	scoreless	redbird	birthday
shorebird	hornbill	cornfed	horsefly

UNIT 15

More Compound Words

Compounds with Vowel-R and Two-Vowel Parts

Compounds with Silent Letter Word Parts

Draw lines between the word parts and decode the words.

downstairs	wristwatch	knockout
outward	eyebrow	kneecap
footsore	flashlight	lighthouse
birdhouse	halfback	knothole
hardwood	penknife	knapsack
bookstore	shipwreck	starlight
whirlpool	midnight	doorjamb
warehouse	knuckleball	wristband
storeroom	highway	highlight
bookmark	moonlight	dogfight
outburst	nightmare	stepdaughter
southward	knockkneed	knighthood
cloudburst	copyright	waistlock
storehouse	thumbnail	thistledown
carpool	whistlestop	sunlight
charcoal	nightgown	slipknot
hoopskirt	bombshell	thumbtack
forestall	calfskin	folktale
spoilsport	thumbprint	dumbbell
airball	playwright	doorknob

UNIT 15

Spelling Vowel-R Compounds

Spell these words that have vowel-r compound parts.

1. _____   2. _____   3. _____

4. _____   5. _____   6. _____

7. _____   8. _____   9. _____

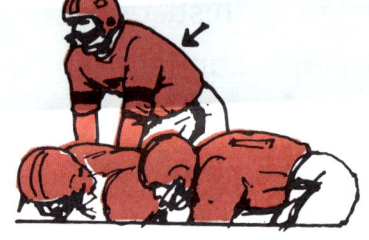

10. _____   11. _____   12. _____

130

Compounds with Sight Word Parts

UNIT 15

These compound words have parts included in the list of 100 sight words that you learned to decode in Units 1 through 8.

Draw lines between the word parts, underline the sight word part, and decode the words.

stepfather	shoestring	doorbell	grandchild
gingerbread	eyeball	outdo	overcome
something	somewhere	somehow	anyhow
anywhere	indoor	forefather	anybody
income	somewhat	output	someone
putout	twosome	headlight	eyebrow
headfirst	eyelash	headlong	eyelid
doorknob	whoever	doorstep	hairdo
today	therefore	comeback	hasbeen
headmaster	wastecan	storefront	doorstop
topmost	somebody	outdoor	godmother
deadbeat	whatever	lovelorn	thoughtless
touchstone	bedroll	underwear	stepchild
hereafter	cocksure	roughhouse	schoolroom
weightless	pullover	horselaugh	piecemeal
washboard	tasteless	fullback	outweigh
doorway	walkway	talkfest	headway
workman	breakfast	throughout	watchdog
somewhat	friendless	yourself	foremost
	livelong	otherwise	tonight

131

UNIT 15

Reading Sentences

If the sentence is true, draw a circle around **T**. If it is not true, circle the **F**.

1. Locksmiths do not understand how to open a padlock on a strongbox.   T   F
2. Blacksmiths are not needed to fit horseshoes at racetracks today.   T   F
3. Thunderstorms and overcast skies slow aircraft takeoffs from airport runways.   T   F
4. Some motormen on downtown streetcars use sunglasses to soften the sunlight.   T   F
5. Schoolboys and their classmates are forbidden to play baseball or football on freshly blacktopped schoolyards.   T   F
6. A good craftsman has to have a blueprint to make a pigsty in a barnyard.   T   F
7. A sawmill owner might make plywood baseboards from hardwood sawdust.   T   F
8. A skindiver in a rowboat needs a waterproof raincoat in a cloudburst at the seashore.   T   F
9. A shiftless workman might do a slipshod job making a playground sandbox.   T   F
10. A rich grandmother might give a friendless stepchild a wristwatch on her birthday.   T   F
11. Could anyone foretell that airplanes would take the place of railroads and steamboats in your grandfather's lifetime?   T   F
12. A careless oarsman in a rowboat could somehow lose an oar in midstream.   T   F
13. A football team's star halfback would spend most of the afternoon on the sidelines.   T   F
14. A fisherman who wants to catch starfish should bait his fishhook with peanut butter.   T   F
15. Anyone who wants to proofread roadside billboards must have flawless eyesight.   T   F

132

UNIT 15

Reading Sentences

Draw a line under **yes** or **no**.

1. Would someone see cowboys on horseback roping longhorns at roundups? Yes No
2. Would the brakemen on railroad boxcars be wearing handsome neckties? Yes No
3. Could a baseball shortstop make a shoestring catch barehanded for a putout? Yes No
4. Could you and your classmates use looseleaf notebooks in your schoolroom? Yes No
5. Did our forefathers meet warlike frontiersmen when they moved westward? Yes No
6. Must the storerooms in warehouses be soundproof? Yes No
7. Does one still see many windmills and scarecrows in barnyards today? Yes No
8. Could a hitchhiker on the highway or turnpike use an oilskin raincoat during a cloudburst? Yes No
9. Could the quarterback on a football club be returning the kickoff for his teammates? Yes No
10. Did backwoods housewives need cornmeal to make pancakes on their cookstoves? Yes No
11. Would anybody need a bookkeeper to keep track of textbooks in a classroom? Yes No
12. Would grapefruit and oatmeal make a good breakfast for your grandfather? Yes No
13. Could anyone get a passport from a salesman in a hardware store? Yes No
14. Would bluebirds and woodpeckers sometimes live in the same birdhouse? Yes No
15. Would you see sandboxes and seesaws in schoolyard playgrounds? Yes No

UNIT 16

Dividing Words into Parts

Many two-syllable words have a vowel letter, two consonant letters, and a vowel letter—the VCCV pattern.

Divide the word between the two consonant letters. Sound out both word parts to say the word.

VC|CV
com|mon

VC|CV
at|tend

We usually say one word part louder than the other part. We say—

COMmon

atTEND

When we say a word part softly, we change the vowel sound. Instead of saying /a/ or /e/ or /i/ or /o/ or /u/, we say a soft "uh" sound. The dictionary shows this soft sound with an upside-down e. It is called a *schwa* /ə/. The dictionary shows a louder word part with a *stress*, or *accent* mark.

kom'ən/

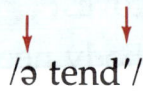
/ə tend'/

Draw a line between the consonant letters in these VCCV words. Sound out the parts. Say the word correctly. Put a stress mark on the louder word part.

| lesson | yellow | mammal | sudden | suppose |
| traffic | raccoon | flatten | surround | tunnel |

134

VCCV Words

Draw lines between the consonants. Place stress marks on the loud syllable. Decode the words.

effort	druggist	cellar	shallow	manner
maggot	dummy	scaffold	pepper	arrest
struggle	village	summit	collide	written
willow	errand	supply	kennel	dessert
offer	funny	collect	correct	announce
differ	glutton	supper	fossil	scatter
mirror	happen	follow	shellac	dipper
gladden	gully	sorrow	flannel	mellow
chatter	pattern	pellet	support	copper
cobbler	cotton	quarry	message	sadden
collar	tennis	minnow	account	annoy
coffin	happy	attend	rubbish	robber
common	comment	gallop	quarrel	appoint
cottage	tassel	attic	mutton	stagger
command	lobby	lesson	channel	middle
connect	fellow	hollow	oppose	rally
cunning	accuse	attack	tallow	skinny
current	muffin	sudden	terrace	kettle
derrick	bottom	succeed	suggest	barrel
stucco	summer	coffee	hiccup	bonnet
taffy	gallon	blossom	burrow	gizzard
skillet	rotten	furrow	attempt	penny
tattoo	motto	traffic	cabbage	pummel
hidden	hello	borrow	blizzard	grammar
afford	gossip	lasso	banner	Jello

UNIT 16

Spelling VCCV Words

Spell these VCCV Words.

1. _____ 2. _____ 3. _____

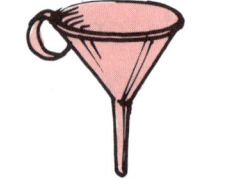  

4. _____ 5. _____ 6. _____

 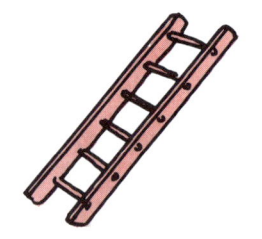 

7. _____ 8. _____ 9. _____

10. _____ 11. _____ 12. _____

  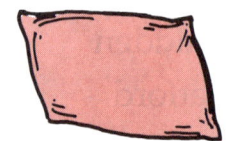

13. _____ 14. _____ 15. _____

UNIT 16

More VCCV Patterns

Many VCCV words have two different consonant letters inside the words. We divide the words between the consonant letters.

VC|CV
nap|kin

VC|CV
per|haps

Draw lines between the consonant letters.
Place accent marks on the louder syllable.
Decode the words.

cartoon	garden	napkin	market	plastic
hermit	silver	enjoy	margin	temper
splendid	ignite	velvet	admire	serpent
argue	circus	kidnap	suspect	transom
indeed	forlorn	lumber	harbor	selfish
varnish	bargain	scarlet	picnic	publish
contest	turnip	catsup	rescue	oblong
person	harness	cluster	subject	sherbet
dentist	marvel	fountain	winter	musket
mistake	garbage	curfew	badger	mascot
seldom	cargo	bamboo	chapter	stampede
costume	insist	orbit	sharpen	husband
escape	pardon	carton	garlic	furnish
elbow	bronco	invite	sputnik	burden
tadpole	entire	public	absent	charcoal
burlap	problem	object	witness	custard
kernel	always	perfect	whisper	inquire
carpet	lawyer	servant	sermon	sentence
admit	canvas	signal	permit	banjo
advice	custom	pencil	goblin	fender

137

UNIT 16

Spelling VCCV Words

Spell these VCCV Words.

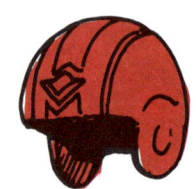 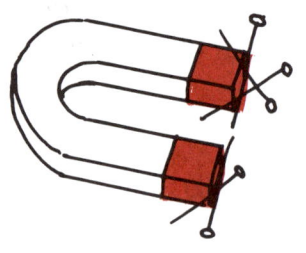 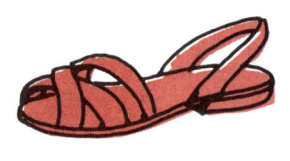

1. _____   2. _____   3. _____

4. _____   5. _____   6. _____

7. _____   8. _____   9. _____

10. _____   11. _____   12. _____

13. _____   14. _____   15. _____

UNIT 16

The V/CV Spelling Pattern

Other words have a vowel-consonant-vowel pattern. We often divide the word *before* the consonant letter. This is the V/CV pattern.

In the V/CV pattern, the first syllable ends with a vowel letter. A syllable that ends with a vowel is an "open" syllable. The vowel letter then spells the "long" vowel sound, as in *me*, *go*, *by*, etc.

V|CV	V|CV	V|CV	V|CV	V|CV
la|bel	be|long	pi|lot	o|pen	pu|pil

Draw a line *before* the consonant letter. Decode the words.

human	because	female	fever
vacant	bonus	minus	yoyo
total	faucet	sober	final
notice	duty	cocoa	totem
virus	slogan	siren	below
bacon	hobo	recess	local
razor	oval	radar	rumor
climate	sausage	sedan	cocoon
event	humid	paper	beware
beside	solo	odor	donate
locust	secure	tidy	equip
beyond	provide	stupid	decent
silent	tulip	behave	mason
navy	student	raisin	legal
spider	moment	raven	oboe
beneath	sinus	clover	rotate
hotel	silo	motel	weasel
music	debate	polite	plumage
frozen	private	cement	floral
tiger	poison	before	tripod

UNIT 16

Spelling V/CV Words

Spell these V/CV Words.

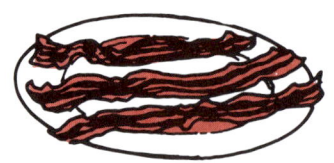

1. _____   2. _____   3. _____

4. _____   5. _____   6. _____

7. _____   8. _____   9. _____

10. _____   11. _____   12. _____

The VC/V Pattern

We divide some VCV words after the consonant letter. This is the VC/V pattern.

When we divide after the consonant letter, the first syllable will end with a consonant letter. A syllable that ends with a consonant letter is a "closed" syllable. The vowel will then spell the "short" sound.

VC|V
trav|el

VC|V
med|al

VC|V
lim|it

VC|V
mod|est

VC|V
pun|ish

Draw a line *after* the consonant letter. Decode the words.

seven	panic	palace	camel
present	menu	wizard	mimic
finish	method	proper	never
wagon	shadow	prison	tenant
rapid	cabin	shiver	relish
forest	damage	satin	tepid
divide	desert	comic	ravel
chisel	modern	comet	topic
polish	closet	second	liver
credit	widow	solid	tonic
timid	gravel	sever	civic
melon	lemon	petal	covet
metal	vanish	pivot	divot
given	linen	driven	basil
model	coward	clinic	docile
disease	dragon	famish	navel
salad	body	lever	tenor
robin	level	snivel	senate
radish	lizard	driver	devil
planet	manage	rivet	pedal

UNIT 16

Spelling VC/V Words

Spell these VC/V Words.

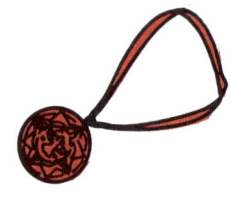

1. _____ 2. _____ 3. _____

4. _____ 5. _____ 6. _____

7. _____ 8. _____ 9. _____

10. _____ 11. _____ 12. _____

142

UNIT 16

Reading VCV and VCCV Sentences

If the sentence is true, mark **T**. If it is false, mark **F**.

1. Many pilots have flown to distant planets.   T   F
2. Human diseases can be caused by a virus.   T   F
3. It is the duty of the navy to protect our shores.   T   F
4. Some pupils attend private schools.   T   F
5. Most frozen polar lands have humid climates.   T   F
6. Athletes always manage to become model students.   T   F
7. Music programs are always open to the public.   T   F
8. Motels and hotels like to hire polite workers.   T   F
9. Some spiders are caught in linen closets.   T   F
10. Gravel and cement are hauled in sedans.   T   F
11. Metal polish is good for satin dresses.   T   F
12. Clever slogans help merchants sell products.   T   F
13. Cowards who panic are apt to become timid.   T   F
14. Chicks and razor blades are made of metal.   T   F
15. Hoboes like to live in vacant cabins.   T   F
16. Cooks often mix radishes into their salads.   T   F
17. Lizards will never be driven from the deserts.   T   F
18. Model prisons are supposed to be secure.   T   F
19. Female robins have more sober plumage than the males.   T   F
20. Famished people should have credit to buy food.   T   F

UNIT 16

VCCCV Words and Three-Syllable Words

The VCCCV Pattern

Some words have three consonant letters between two vowel letters. We divide most of these VCCCV words after the first consonant letter.

Divide these VCCCV words into syllables by drawing a line after the first consonant letter. Decode the words.

pilgrim	central
address	thirsty
ostrich	attract
tantrum	emblem
surplus	monster
nostril	employ
children	distress
lobster	embrace
merchant	burglar
perspire	control
hamster	entrance
frustrate	dandruff
mattress	pantry
laundry	concrete
tumbler	belfry
orchard	display
sentry	district
purchase	sultry
surprise	gastric
hundred	paltry

Dividing Three-Syllable Words

Three-syllable words often have the common V/CV, VC/V and VC/CV divisions. Draw lines between the word parts, or syllables in these words. Decode the words.

tomato	cucumber
absolute	mandolin
porcupine	committee
torpedo	octopus
ambulance	molasses
bulletin	buffalo
circulate	moccasin
elastic	opposite
pendulum	accurate
tornado	ignorant
gymnastics	advertise
carpenter	fantastic
acrobat	antelope
volcano	hibernate
potato	suffocate
calculate	domestic
barbecue	establish
sarcastic	utensil
abdomen	appetite
occupy	sacrifice
tobacco	indignant
percolate	consonant
alcohol	adventure
balcony	occupant

UNIT 16

Spelling Three-Syllable Words

Say the three syllables clearly. Spell the parts to make one word.

1. _____ 2. _____ 3. _____

 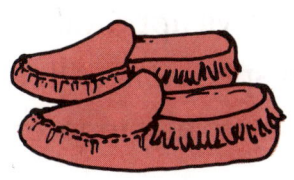 

4. _____ 5. _____ 6. _____

  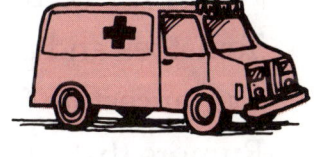

7. _____ 8. _____ 9. _____

  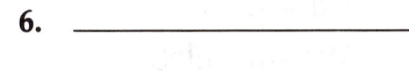

10. _____ 11. _____ 12. _____

UNIT 16

Reading Long Word Sentences

If the sentence is true, mark T. If it is false, mark F.

1.	Impudent students are sometimes impolite to their professors.	T	F
2.	Large committees should be employed to supervise factory workers.	T	F
3.	Porcupines suffocate if they try to hibernate.	T	F
4.	Doctors normally operate on one's appendix in the hospital.	T	F
5.	Carpenters who make and paint furniture use turpentine.	T	F
6.	Modern astronauts have had fantastic adventures.	T	F
7.	City inspectors are needed to give approval to electric wiring.	T	F
8.	Clever acrobats can entertain spectators with daring gymnastics.	T	F
9.	Attorneys are rarely needed by totally innocent citizens accused of crimes.	T	F
10.	Candidates for public office ought to advertise in church bulletins.	T	F
11.	We still celebrate President Washington's birthday.	T	F
12.	People are accustomed to have a dictator rule a democracy.	T	F
13.	Tomatoes and potatoes are commonly cooked in casseroles.	T	F
14.	Our ancestors founded our republic less than a century ago.	T	F
15.	Rumors that circulate rapidly tend to be accurate.	T	F
16.	People from abroad often develop an appetite for our domestic barbecue.	T	F
17.	There are sound arguments against the use of tobacco and alcohol.	T	F
18.	Moccasins can be made from the hides of antelopes and buffalo.	T	F
19.	Generals outrank corporals in the military.	T	F
20.	Dinosaurs still terrorize natives near the equator.	T	F

Prefixes, Roots, and Suffixes

Prefixes

A prefix is a word part we place at the beginning of a word or a word root. Like words, prefixes have meaning. When we place a prefix in front of a known English word, the prefix changes the meaning of the word. Prefixes appear in front of word roots, which are usually Latin word parts.

The prefix **re** means "back," or "again." **Repay** means to "pay back." **Recount** means to "count again."

The prefix **ex** means "from," or "out." To **export** means to "send out" or "from."

$$re = \begin{matrix} \text{back} \\ \text{again} \end{matrix}$$

$$ex = \begin{matrix} \text{out} \\ \text{from} \end{matrix}$$

EXAMPLES:

repay   recount

EXAMPLE:

export

Draw lines between the prefixes and the roots. Decode the words.

recall	return	express	excuse
remind	replace	expose	exhale
regain	reclaim	explain	exile
recross	rejoin	exchange	extend
rename	repaid	exclaim	expand
reload	reread	exceed	expend
replant	retrace	excel	expire
rebound	refresh	except	explore
refill	refund	excite	extract
reprint	resist	exclude	explode

Com and Con Prefixes

UNIT 17

Draw lines between the prefixes and roots. Decode the words.

The prefix **com** has the same meaning as the prefix **con**—"with," or "together." **Combat** is to "fight with." **Compress** is to "press together."

              with
com =
              together

EXAMPLES:

combat   **compress**

compact	compute	command
compose	compare	commence
compound	compel	comfort
combine	compete	comment
commit	commune	company
complain	commend	compare

The prefix **con** means "with" or "together." To **conspire** means to "plot with."

              with
con =
              together

EXAMPLE:

conspire

confirm	conspire	conclude
confine	conceal	confer
conform	console	confess
condense	consent	confide
convince	concern	confuse
consider	consist	consult

UNIT 17

Dis and De Prefixes

Draw lines between the prefixes and roots.
Decode the words.

The prefix **dis** usually gives the meaning of "opposite." So, **dislike** is the opposite of the root word like.

dis = opposite

EXAMPLE:

dislike

disown	discolor	dislike
discover	dismount	displace
disloyal	disarm	disagree
disprove	disorder	discard
displease	distrust	discharge
discount	disclaim	dislodge

The prefix **de** means "down," or "from," or "away." **Depart** means to "go from" or "away." **Depress** means to "press down."

          down
de = from
          away

EXAMPLES:

depart   **depress**

deform	descend	defeat
degrade	decline	deflate
define	decode	describe
depress	decrease	depose
detest	defame	defrost
detain	default	deflect

Pro, Pre, and Im Prefixes

UNIT 17

The prefix **pro** often means, "for," or "onward." A **pronoun** "stands for a noun." To **promote** means to "move onward."

pro = for / onward

EXAMPLES:

pronoun   **promote**

The prefix **pre** means "before." We "fix" a **prefix** "before" a word root.

pre = before

EXAMPLE:

prefix

The prefix **im** means "not." **Impolite** means "not polite." The **im** may also mean "in." **Implant** means to "plant in."

im = not / in

EXAMPLES:

impolite   **implant**

Draw lines between the prefixes and roots. Decode the words.

pronoun	prepaid	impress
protest	precede	impure
provide	precook	improper
propose	predate	impolite
proceed	predict	impersonal
proclaim	prefab	imperfect
procure	prefer	immortal
produce	prefix	immodest
profess	prejudge	immense
profile	preflight	immerse
profuse	prepare	improval
program	prepay	imprudent
prohibit	preschool	implore
prolong	preshrunk	import
pronounce	presume	impose
propel	pretend	imprint
protrude	pretest	imprison
provoke	prevail	implicate

150

UNIT 17

En, In, and Un Prefixes

The prefix **en**, like **in**, means "in, into, make." **Enclose** means "close in." **Endanger** means "put into danger." **Enable** means "make able."

en = in / into / make

EXAMPLES:

enclose enable endanger

The prefix **in** sometimes means "in," sometimes "not." **Inlaid** means "laid in." **Insane** means "not sane."

in = in / not

EXAMPLES:

inlaid insane

The prefix **un** means "not," or "opposite." **Unhappy** means "not happy." **Unlock** is the opposite of lock.

on = not / opposite

EXAMPLES:

unhappy unlock

Draw lines between the prefixes and roots. Decode the words.

entrust	income	unpack
enlist	inclose	unripe
enclose	indent	unsound
enrich	indoor	untold
enrage	inform	unfold
endear	inborn	unclean
encase	incline	unjust
enact	include	untie
endorse	invest	unload
enfold	induce	unsafe
engage	inflate	unwire
enjoy	inhabit	untried
enlarge	inhuman	unfit
enroll	insecure	uneasy
entwine	insert	unarmed
entrench	inspire	unsure
enthuse	insult	uncut
engulf	invent	unfair

151

Suffixes

A suffix is a word part we place at the end of a word or word root. Most suffixes do not change the root meanings, as prefixes do. Noun suffixes change words into nouns. Adjective suffixes change words into adjective forms. Some suffixes are both noun and adjective suffixes.

We use the suffix **–ness** to change words into nouns. We change **good** to **goodness**, **weak** to **weakness**, etc.

–ness

We use the suffix **–tion** to make nouns. We change **act** to **action**, **elect** to **election**, etc.

–tion

We use the **–ment** suffix to form nouns. We add **ment** to **agree** to make **agreement**, to **amuse** to make **amusement**, etc.

–ment

EXAMPLES: EXAMPLES: EXAMPLES:

goodness   weakness   action   election   agreement   amusement

Draw lines between the suffixes and roots. Decode the words.

richness	motion	payment
greatness	portion	placement
sickness	station	shipment
likeness	lotion	ornament
madness	suction	movement
illness	action	treatment
sadness	fraction	statement
sweetness	friction	settlement
dampness	section	argument
stillness	nation	enjoyment
darkness	vacation	torment
thickness	fiction	garment
fondness	mention	judgment
quickness	notion	comment
firmness	election	parchment
soundness	collection	assortment

UNIT 17

Suffixes -ance, -ence, and -ant

Draw lines between the suffixes and the roots.
Decode the words.

We use the suffix **–ance** to make nouns. We change **allow** to **allowance**, **assist** to **assistance**, etc.

–ance

EXAMPLES:

allowance   **assistance**

balance	clearance	elegance
distance	allowance	tolerance
instance	appearance	hesitance
annoyance	fragrance	semblance
assistance	temperance	entrance
ignorance	arrogance	finance

The suffix **–ence** is also used to make nouns.

–ence

EXAMPLE:

difference

sentence	difference	residence
presence	evidence	persistence
silence	diligence	negligence
absence	innocence	eloquence
offense	permanence	reverence
defense	turbulence	penitence

The suffix **–ant** is used to form nouns or adjectives. We change **please** to **pleasant**, **serve** to **servant**, etc.

–ant

EXAMPLES:

pleasant   **servant**

gallant	stagnant	applicant
vacant	pennant	occupant
distant	instant	significant
merchant	hesitant	assistant
warrant	tolerant	ignorant
servant	fragnant	elegant

Like **ant**, the suffix **–ent** forms nouns or adjectives. We change **differ** to **different**, **preside** to **president**, etc.

–ent

EXAMPLES:

different   **president**

silent	frequent	opponent
decent	absent	different
recent	content	accident
student	serpent	negligent
talent	insolent	turbulent
current	torrent	evident

Suffixes -ful, -able, -ible, and -ous

Draw lines between the suffixes and roots. Decode the words.

The **–ful** suffix is used to make adjectives or nouns. We change **care** to **careful**, **arm** to **armful**.

–ful

EXAMPLES:

careful   **armful**

graceful	faithful	careful
lawful	tactful	grateful
harmful	hopeful	helpful
useful	spiteful	joyful
fearful	painful	playful
skillful	cheerful	restful

We use the suffix **–able** to form adjectives. We change **agree** to **agreeable**, **honor** to **honorable**, etc.

–able

EXAMPLES:

agreeable   **honorable**

agreeable	reasonable	favorable
teachable	miserable	portable
washable	enjoyable	acceptable
passable	perishable	advisable
notable	suitable	peaceable
workable	readable	durable

We use the **–ible** suffix also to form adjectives.

–ible

EXAMPLE:

forcible

sensible	edible	plausible
possible	audible	collapsible
visible	legible	divisible
terrible	tangible	permissible
flexible	forcible	negligible
horrible	digestible	

We use the **–ous** suffix to form adjectives. We change **fame** to **famous**, **danger** to **dangerous**.

–ous

EXAMPLES:

famous   **dangerous**

joyous	jealous	vigorous
nervous	marvelous	famous
callous	numerous	fabulous
odorous	curious	humorous
perilous	glorious	generous
harazdous	poisonous	tremendous

UNIT 17

Suffixes -less, -ive, and -al

Draw lines between the suffixes and the roots. Decode the words.

We use the **–less** suffix to change nouns into adjectives. We add **less** to **pain** to form **painless**.

–less

EXAMPLE:

painless

useless	helpless	groundless
fearless	homeless	aimless
harmless	stainless	cloudless
thoughtless	hopeless	toothless
careless	lawless	aimless
restless	thankless	spotless

We use the **–ive** suffix to change nouns and verbs into adjectives. We add **ive** to **act** to form **active**.

–ive

EXAMPLE:

active

massive	attentive	talkative
cursive	attractive	offensive
motive	sensitive	successive
passive	positive	selective
elusive	elective	negative
active	furtive	objective

We use the **–al** suffix to change nouns and verbs into adjectives. We add **al** to form **musical**.

–al

EXAMPLE:

musical

formal	central	vocal
comical	global	rural
personal	seasonal	floral
rental	spiral	coastal
brutal	spinal	removal
normal	portal	national

155

UNIT 17

Prefixes, Roots, and Suffixes

We add both prefixes and suffixes to roots to form new words.

PREFIX	+	ROOT	+	SUFFIX	=	WORD
de	+	fend	+	ant	=	defendant
re	+	sist	+	ance	=	resistance
dis	+	trust	+	ful	=	distrustful
im	+	polite	+	ness	=	impoliteness
in	+	differ	+	ence	=	indifference
en	+	force	+	ment	=	enforcement
ex	+	press	+	ive	=	expressive
com	+	fort	+	less	=	comfortless
con	+	ten	+	tion	=	contention
pre	+	ven	+	tion	=	prevention
pro	+	nounce	+	ment	=	pronouncement
un	+	fair	+	ness	=	unfairness
im	+	poss	+	ible	=	impossible
pre	+	fer	+	able	=	preferable
in	+	sol	+	ent	=	insolent
con	+	fid	+	ence	=	confidence
de	+	sir	+	ous	=	desirous

UNIT 17

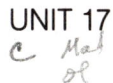

Prefixes, Roots, and Suffixes

Draw lines between the prefixes, roots, and suffixes. Decode the words.

reappearance	refreshment	construction
department	description	preferment
disgraceful	unemployment	protective
important	protection	unskillful
instruction	prejudgment	reflection
enrollment	contestant	development
excellence	competent	disappointment
comfortable	excitement	imprisonment
confidence	enforcible	intention
predictable	informant	engagement
probation	impulsive	enrollment
unsuitable	disagreeable	combatant
exception	reception	contentment
compartment	dependence	pronouncement
inhabitant	displacement	ungenerous
continent	imprudent	delightful
progressive	investment	retirement
envious	enjoyable	preventable
deliverance	expensive	impersonal
impossible	commandment	dismissal